ALIENS IN OUR MIDST

ALIENS IN OUR MIDST

The Ancients

asemic writings 1

Mark Urizar
Zbigniew Jaworski

To order additional copies of this book, contact:
Xlibris
AU TFN: 1 800 844 927 (Toll Free inside Australia)
AU Local: (02) 8310 8187 (+61 2 8310 8187 from outside Australia)
www.Xlibris.com.au
Orders@Xlibris.com.au
849055

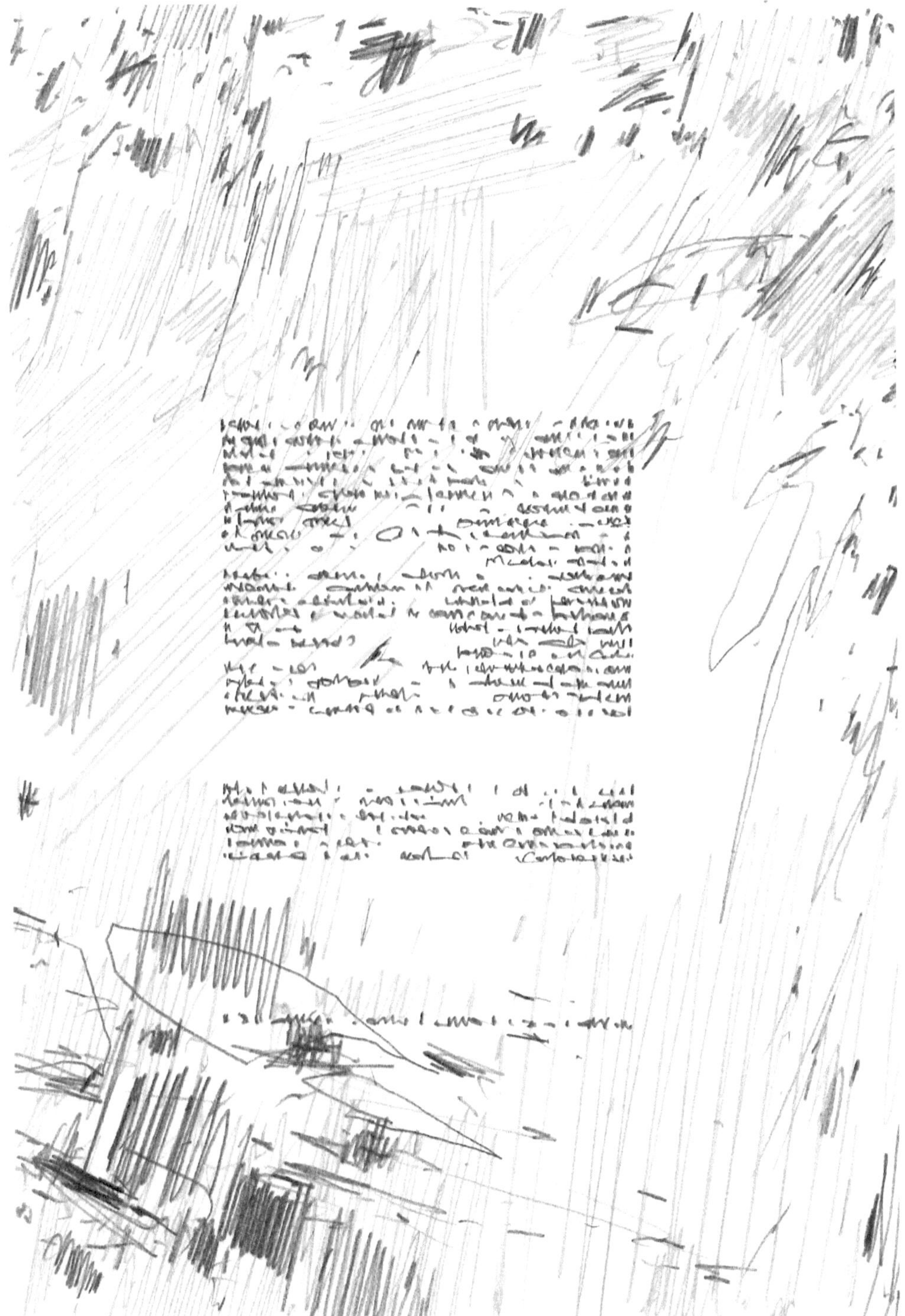

*All that we believe and think to be real and true is about to change.
The previously discarded fictional, strange, and disturbingly insane has begun
to permeate into our reality and is revealing its own truth.*

CONTENTS

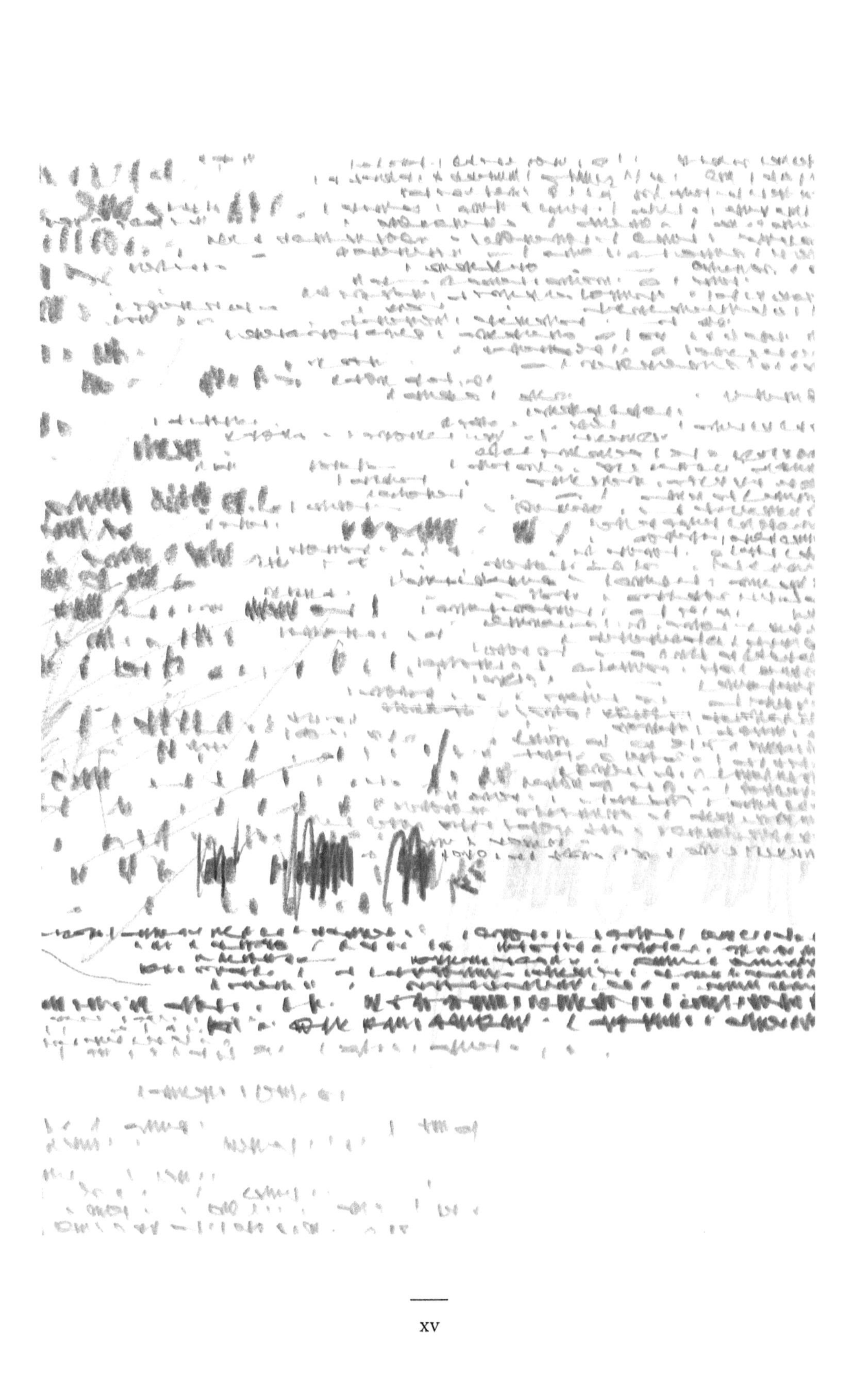

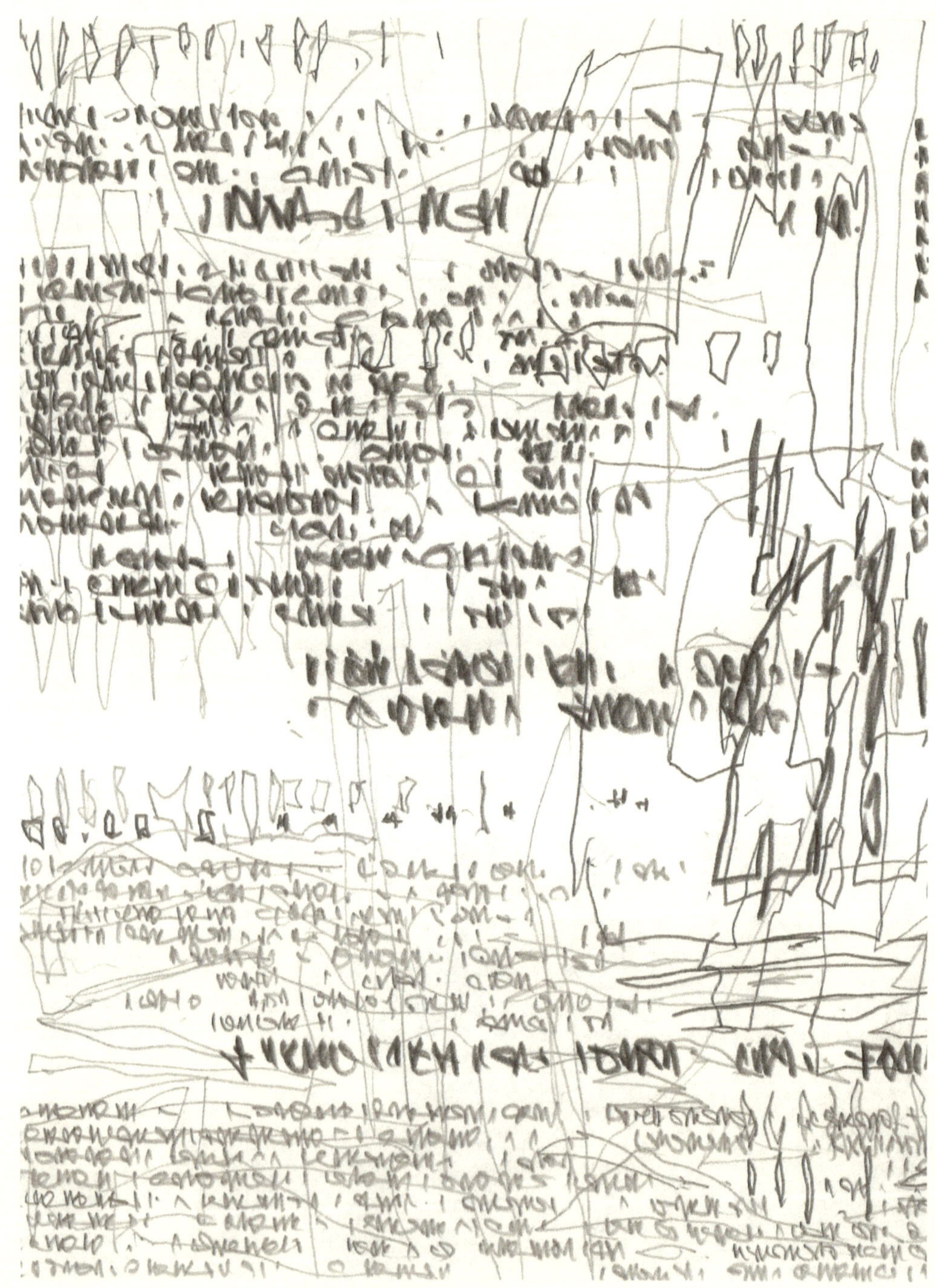

Foreword

What links Einstein with dinosaurs, a sixty-three-million-year-long Mayan calendar, and aliens?

There are many obscure yet inconceivable links that tie this reality with the incomprehensible and strange. Some are well beyond reason or understanding, and yet these inevitably and nevertheless exist.

Without a second thought, we readily discard all we disbelieve along with the improbable and strange. Without us realising, our minds are regularly outsmarted. A preconditioning exists that diverts or constrains our thoughts so to limit what we perceive. To reawaken, we must dispel this cast spell with its limitations. To do so, we will need to accept we lack imagination with understanding of all there is. We also will need the courage to venture deep within our minds so we can find answers to our past and all the previously forbidden questions. As these shifts and sways our thinking and reframes our reality, eventually, it will reveal all that was previously hidden in plain sight. We will then see the inconceivable and improbable and, with these, find the most elusive answers and simplest and indivisible truths.

This is how truth emerges. It waits for a receptive mind to seep into and fill so to manifest into existence. When it is ripe and ready, it wafts in, attaches and transcribes itself to visceral feelings with its otherwise expressionless, meaningless language. As it dwells there, the substance it gains provides glimpses of its own, unique reality. This blurs and merges the distinction between what is real and not, crystalising to expose a strangeness with clarity that brings its own truth. This then cannot be unseen, overlooked, manipulated, or changed as this is the truth that will remain so – forevermore.

THE STRANGE REALITY

How strange can the truth and reality be?

We are conceited if we think we are it. Earth's history is long and complex, and the evolution of life has not been straightforward. We have lived only for the briefest moment, the shortest fraction of Earth's history. We became because all that previously existed perished. We are not the first, and nor will we be the last. We are not the most evolved or the most intelligent that ever lived. We are mere newcomers, having recently arrived and begun our journey.

An obscure and inexplicably deep past exists that is well beyond our visual horizon or mental comprehension. We are fooled if we think there is a simple or straight-line evolution from primate to caveman and then to the AMH (anatomically modern human). Earth's fractured evolutionary history has been purposefully doctored and diluted, with parts changed to suit a distorted world view created for mass public consumption. It is this that still separates humanity from all that extends well beyond us,

the indivisible truth.

All There Ever Was and Is

What has been shall be. What has been done will be done. There is nothing new under the sun. (Ecclesiastes)

This sacred Old Testament scripture is not fatalistic but ordained. It sets how destiny unfolds. All life is tied to its past and destined to repeat what has already occurred. We therefore are too destined to experience all that came before us. If we are fortunate, we will not repeat past mistakes.

We can learn from the past, from **history**, as it continually repeats. What has occurred will occur.

Simply peering back in time reveals what is likely to occur. This, we cannot change. Nor can we stop what is already in motion. All we can do is improve from the past by avoiding the mistakes our predecessors made and by preparing for what is already destined to occur and come.

Within this lies the repetitive cycle of life, which gives us only one chance to succeed. This is our lives' challenge. We cannot try again by rewinding time. Life is not a computer simulation. Life can only be lived once. This is all providence provides. To persist and succeed, we must therefore prepare for the worst, the unthinkable, the calamities that are yet to come while we endure lives monotonies. If we fail to prepare, our inactions will strand us in time and prevent us from reaching or realising our destiny.

The Cycle of Life

There exists an incomprehensible yet pure essence of intelligence that is everywhere. It is ubiquitous. It is within all matter and life. This is what initially brought atoms together and then created systems and places so life could manifest and exist on this plane. This is also what pulsed at **creation** and set the universal beat with its unending cycles of renewal that progresses and evolves life to some end.

We became because of this. This cyclical renewal process gave us this temporary form and eventually, it will also take this from us, as it recycles, renews and progresses life to its next level.

The cycle of life will eventually recycle and renew everything – trees, animals, people, stars, and even gods. This is how life persists, evolves, and how it is to fulfil its destiny.

Ordained, this cannot be changed. But by knowing this, we should be comforted by what humanity has already achieved and consider the time already granted to us as a blessing, as we were not owed a living or an existence. We are merely one insignificant species within the large scheme of things, having lived for a momentary blip in time, during the shortest epoch of Earth's history, and the smallest part of one cycle within a large ocean of time. And like all other species, we are given one opportunity to succeed, to fulfil our destiny, before this relentless cycle turns again. When this occurs, it will then inevitably progress past us by resetting life, causing a renewal that brings forth a new era with what emerges. This is what has happened countless times before to many species, and is destined to repeat forevermore.

That Night

When the ancients venture, they come to steal our thoughts and souls. No one sees or hears them. They come at night, when we least expect, when everyone is deep in sleep. They manifest suddenly, emerging from thin air, stealthily moving within our midst. With seeming magical powers, they lock our minds, disable our bodies, and take what they want.

This is what happened to me. I was taken that night.

When I regained consciousness, I found myself paralysed, floating upright, unable to move. Then after what seemed an eternity, I saw some seemingly familiar shapes approach. These appeared alien like, who began to move me, taking me past many fantastical, impossible structures, machines, and buildings. This place seemed familiar. I remembered this. I was here before. This was not Earth. I then knew I had been abducted.

Old yet

forgotten

memories flooded my mind. Somehow coming here unblocked these repressed memories from past abductions. I knew then what would occur next, the process. Soon, the operation began. I was unable to move. I felt each and every incision yet without pain. I knew this was my fate, my destiny, which would continue until my end.

Another eternity passed before I was again moved. I was then taken to meet Q. Q is an ageless, all-powerful being. I remembered Q from previous abductions. Q is exceedingly old, predating this galaxy, having lived for billions of years. Q is unlike anything and everything else. As I approached Q, crystal-clear images manifested as thoughts in my mind. This is how Q communicates – no words were exchanged, and yet I understood everything. As we communicated, I felt at peace. I also felt my mind and awareness expand, enabling me to understand all that was previously incomprehensible to me. Soon, I knew and understood everything.

The Awakening and Remembering

I felt strange when I awoke. I was back home.

As the fog of sleep lifted from my mind, I remembered and realised I again had been abducted by the ancients. I pondered for a while. My thoughts lingered on the details of the process with its procedures and operations. Then my thoughts shifted to the conversation I had had with Q. I then realised the significance of this. I could remember and thereby relive every single moment of this encounter. I knew all that I remembered should have been erased. The ancients had always taken this from me – but not this time. For some reason, the ancients and Q had allowed me to retain this memory. They had wanted me to remember.

REMEMBERING

The insight and knowledge I gained from Q had enlightened my life. This is what is written; a tale that does not recount an alien encounter but rather how and why we became human. Intertwined is also the story of life, this universe, this solar system, planet Earth, and the tale of the ancients. This I wrote before amnesia again corrupted and cleared my mind. This was all I had remembered, all now forgotten memories of the ancients.

The Human Quandary — An Apparent Manipulation

Why do the Mayans have a sixty-three-million-year-long calendar?

How did our species produce someone like Einstein? How can our mind glimpse the mechanics of matter, imagine the improbable, and understand the impossible with only thousands of years of evolutionary time? Do we all have an innate ability that grants us access to sacred knowledge? How can our minds think of otherwise incomprehensible things – or has this already been seeded in our minds?

Earth's 4.543 Ga (billion years) age provided ample evolutionary time, with multiple opportunities for intelligent life to manifest into existence. The one species that predated humans gifted with superior intelligence were the ancients. Evolved from an obscure, reptilian-dinosaur form, predating the first mammal by 74 Ma (million years), they had lived on Earth for 9.4 Ma. This evolutionary time they had then **gifted** them the means to exit the cycle of life and become immortals.

They now dwell in the heavens as gods. They influence what occurs on Earth and this universe. With what they do, they have pushed life to its limits so species attained some ultimate form. This is how we became human. The ancients forced evolution on our earliest ancestor: the stem mammal, from which emerged mammals, and then primates, hominids, and hominins and then the AMH.

Who Are the Ancients?

Along the continuum of things, during all of Earth's history, intelligence has always strived to attach itself to life so to realise its destiny.

Intelligence has made us what we are. And it is intelligence that will take us to our destiny. We, as souls in 3-dimensional bodies may live in a larger multi-dimensional world, but only see this reality from the two-dimensional input we receive. We perceive this through a cohesive progression of images, at one plank frame at a time, on a linear time path. By expanding our perception to what is, we begin to sense and realise there are higher, yet traversable realities that hold the promise of connecting us to all there is.

This is what the **ancients** realized and traversed into. It was their psionic abilities that freed them from the grip of the third dimension and enabled them to transcend past the fourth and fifth dimensions. They had used their abilities to elevate themselves above this reality with its material and time limitations, entering an out of phase realm that exists somewhere in the sixth dimension. There, they were able to further enhance their abilities, opening themselves to the seventh dimension and parallel universes. Now, as true outsiders to this plane, from their vantage point, they perceive all there is, the whole chronology of this world, its universe, and multiverses, and as they wish, they can jump anywhere, at any point in time, but still claim to lack the real means to change destined outcomes. Intelligence had enabled them to realise this. This is their tale.

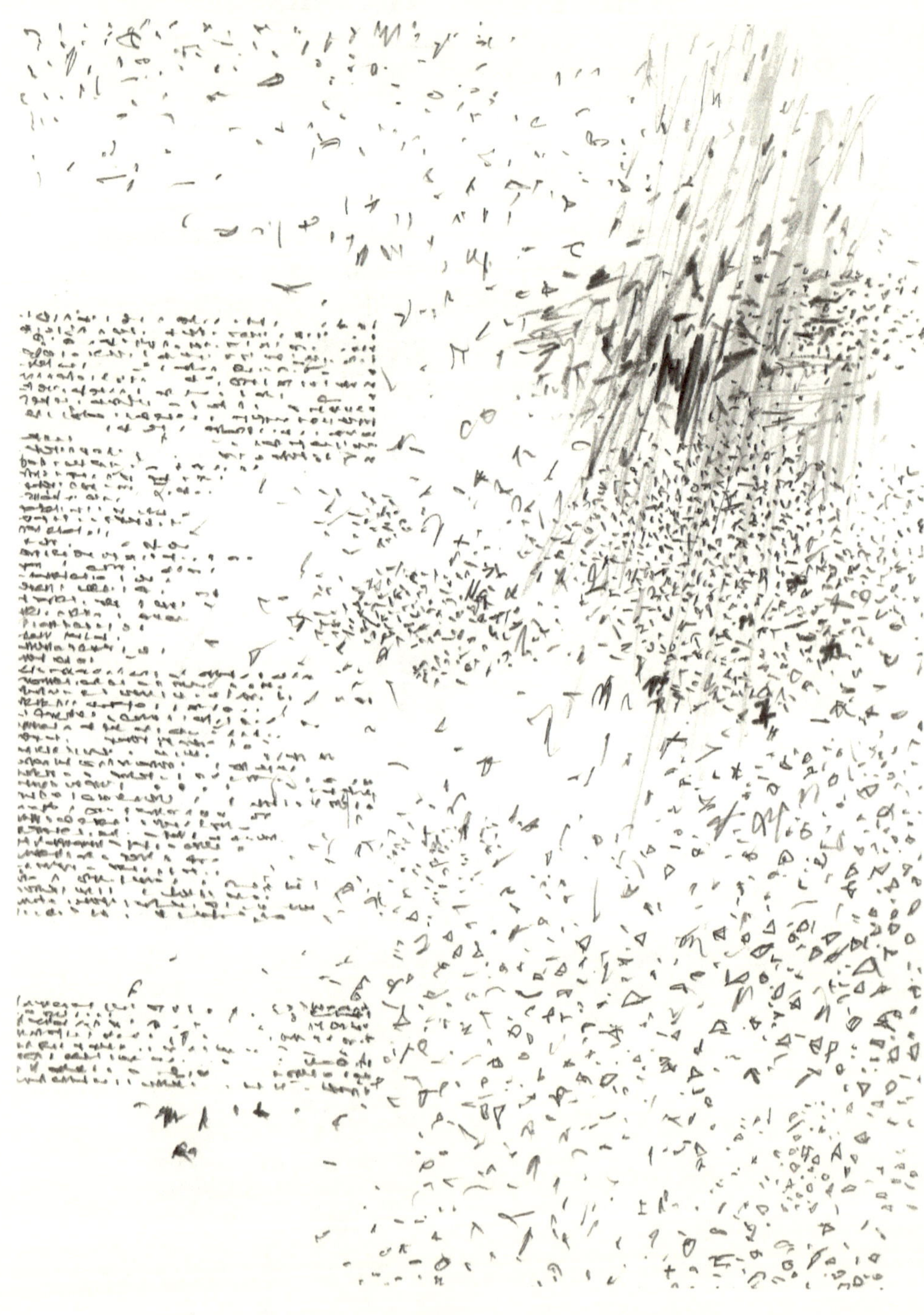

The Abductions

The sixth dimension is an incomprehensible realm. Reality there is altered. Nothing is normal. Everything appears fluid, in a state of flux, including time, space, and matter.

Unlike the third, fourth and fifth dimensions, the sixth is a realm that has arrhythmic cycles with a **resonance** that incessantly reverberates with alternating harmonics and frequencies. There is no real constancy. Even time dilates, slowing and then quickening. Time in the sixth dimension has a visible fluidity that makes it malleable and manipulatable. It can be rewound to past events or extended beyond, into the distant future. A second or minute can be short-lived or extended into days, weeks, months, years, or an eternity.

The resonance within the realm magnifies the mental and innate abilities of mortals. This had gifted the ancients godlike powers; they only need a mere thought to control or manipulate all that exists. With this, the ancients have become master manipulators of space, time and matter.

When they travel, they warp space and so to time their departure with their arrival. They do so to limit the impact on their victims, those they abduct, who only disappear momentarily but are often held for eternity. With this anomaly, no victim can ever fully explain what happened to them.

Q

I had known Q for a long time, possibly for hundreds of years. Q created this out-of-phase realm, manifesting it into existence by a mere thought. Q did this some 6 Ga ago, before this solar system coalesced into existence. This was Q's escape from the turmoil and chaos this universe had undergone at the time when it transitioned into its present form. A dilation occurred that began to implode, compressing and contracting space, pulling galaxies together, causing them to clash incessantly. This nearly ended life in this universe, but fortunately and eventually, the ensuing turmoil eased and calmed, enabling this universe to expand again.

The chaos that consumed and destroyed most of the old then scattered its surviving remnants throughout this universe. These were eventually pulled in by spiralling new and lost suns and newly formed solar systems. This enabled the reset to occur, a rebirth that brought new life to this universe.

Q had manifested its sanctuary to escape the turmoil that ensued from this transition time which then also enabled Q to transcend the **chaos** caused by the reset. Q had used its gifted, extensive psionic abilities to create a time anomaly that then opened portals to a halfway place between the plane of existence and nonexistence, within the sixth dimension. Q restructured space and time so to enable three, four and five-dimensional life to exist there. This then became Q's out-of-phase realm.

Q then waited. It took billions of years for life to again manifest in this universe, followed by further billions of years for it to evolve, mature, and gain sufficient intelligence with psionic abilities. Only the most evolved life gained the means to open portals to Q's realm. From the many beings that have since migrated into this realm, there is only one from Earth: the ancients. They entered this realm 227 Ma ago and since have become integral parts of Q's realm. Their presence, with their contributions, has enabled this realm to flourish and expand.

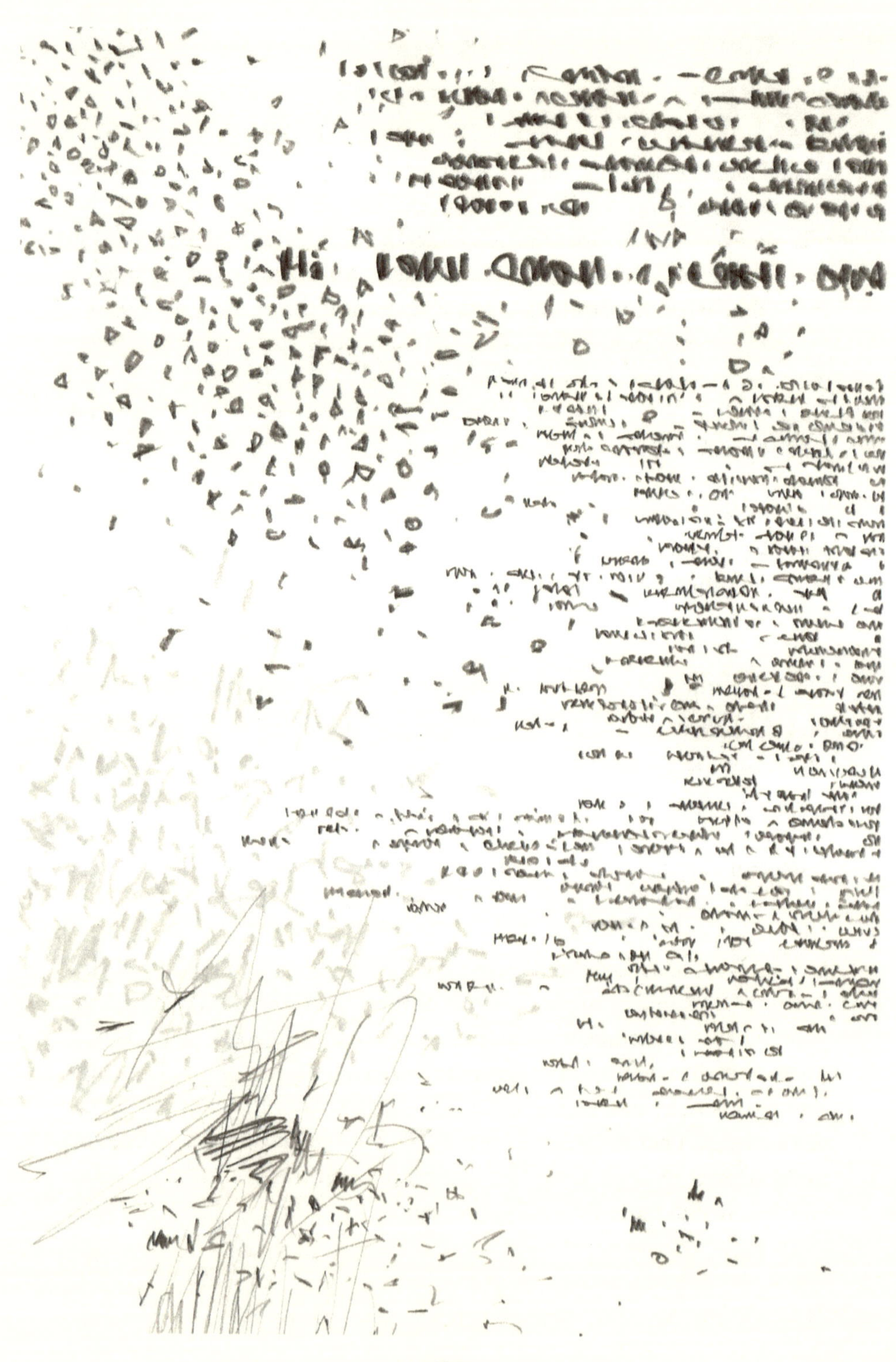

Intelligence

Intelligence is an invisible and formless yet ubiquitous and omnipresent entity. It is eternal, destined to exist forevermore. This is the creator entity. It brought this universe into existence by fracturing and exploding a part of itself into an infinite number of pieces. This caused the big bang and gave form to this universe. It then willed atoms to merge and assemble into particles and matter that became the planets, suns, solar systems, and galaxies. As these formed, the residual intelligence within space tied the whole together so it moved in unison and became one entity with one consciousness.

Intelligence brought this reality into existence with its intent to gain form. All that exists is therefore structured to enable life to manifest and progress so intelligence can one day merge with it and eventually reconnect with its greater consciousness. This is its quest.

We are one of its creations. Our bodies are its vessels. We dwell within its systems, having families and communities, all destined to one day merge as one mind. While intelligence waits for this merge to occur, it has gifted us **intellect and imagination.**

To achieve its quest, intelligence uses the cycle of life with its renewal processes to progress life. What it no longer needs is purposefully devolved and replaced, recycled and exchanged with new, enhanced versions. This, it does with everything that is unnecessary in this universe. In space, it uses black holes to vacuum and distil the wasted matter, devolving it back to its essence and pure intelligence.

Intelligence had taken 4.2 Ga to find its first suitable host on Earth. This, it did with the ancients 237 Ma ago. As it merged with their minds, it gifted them superior intellect and access to a greater consciousness. This eventually would enable the ancients to gain and then expanded their psionic abilities, enabling them to transcend past their mortal existence, exit the cycle of life, and become gods in heaven. We are on the same path. We are destined to gain enhanced abilities that will one day also enable us to transcend past our mortal existence, and when we do, we will then be able to join the ancients in heaven.

The Persistence of Life

Intelligence had created this universe to find its form. At creation, invisible forces began to establish the necessary platforms needed for life to exist. Matter then began appearing from nothingness as the random scatter of atoms merged to create and bring this reality into existence.

Billions of years of iterations followed. Many failed trials became necessary sacrifices, followed a process of cleansing and renewal. This purge of sorts led to much of the early universe being destroyed so to be recycled and reconfigured to an improved version. The life that had failed to progress was then scattered, seeded throughout this universe. This made life ubiquitous, ensuring it would manifest into existence at each opportunity, and what then did emerge was sufficiently resilient so to persist and endure the ensuing chaos and turmoil that would follow the forming of **habitable worlds.**

This is how this universe gifted life to Earth. Many parts of the early destroyed universe landed here, seeding life and enabling it to manifest at its first opportunity. It only took 800 Ma after Earth had formed for life to manifest on the surface, seemingly immediately after it had sufficiently cooled, and once life had gained its foothold here, it then could not be extinguished.

Life on Earth has since progressed through a series of random yet pre-orchestrated events. Each pushed life to its limits so to gain resilience and greater complexity. Each step also quickened and accelerated the evolutionary processes, so what emerged had the drive to attain its most advanced form. From this emerged new, enhanced creations, each an improvement on all that previously existed.

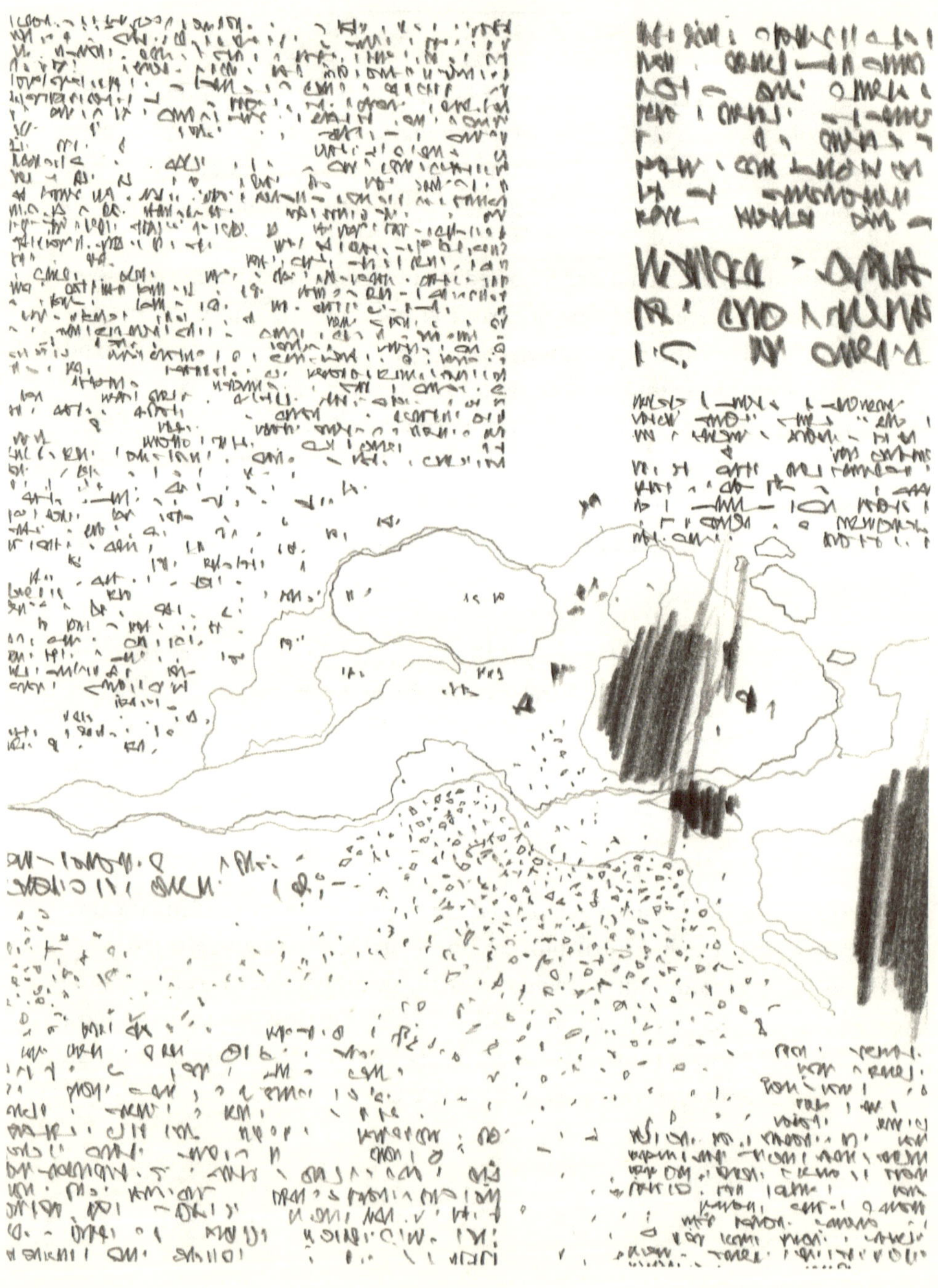

The Apathetic Earth

Our potential is unlimited. We have a mind with an equal number of neurons as all the stars in all the galaxies in this universe. Our mind has the DNA with genetic makeup to realise all there is, but we are limited, constrained to 10 per cent of our potential. The rest lies dormant within. This, we must wait for providence to open and awaken so to also fulfil our destiny. Presently limited are all our thoughts, all governed with false logic and a doctored rationality that simply cannot grapple or comprehend or accept the unthinkable or fantastical as reality. This has bound and dampened our creativity and imagination with the physical and ordinary. This simplifies what we perceive so to also shield us from what we don't understand. We may consider where we are, what we stand on, as inert matter and even consider Earth as a benign being. We think this because we wish it were true. The opposite means Earth is alive. It has its own consciousness, it has intelligence, and it is not a benign being.

Earth manifested into existence pulsing with anger. Fortunately for life on its surface, it has an extreme slow-paced pulse, taking hundreds of millions of years for it to react and unleash its wrath. This, it had done numerous times with its calamitous tantrums causing mass extinctions, but rather than extinguish life, each of these resets led to a rebirth that progressed life. Each had pushed life to its limits, forced it to diversify and diverge, gain complexity, and become sufficiently resilient so to better endure such events.

Extinction events

Time has since mellowed Earth. It now accepts life cannot be extinguished from its surface. It had felt how life was reset by each of its tantrums, only to cause a rebirth and bring forth new growth with new eras. With each, it knew the life that emerged had greater resilience and could thrive and persist through all such adversity. Accepting this, Earth became the apathetic habitable world that we all now populate.

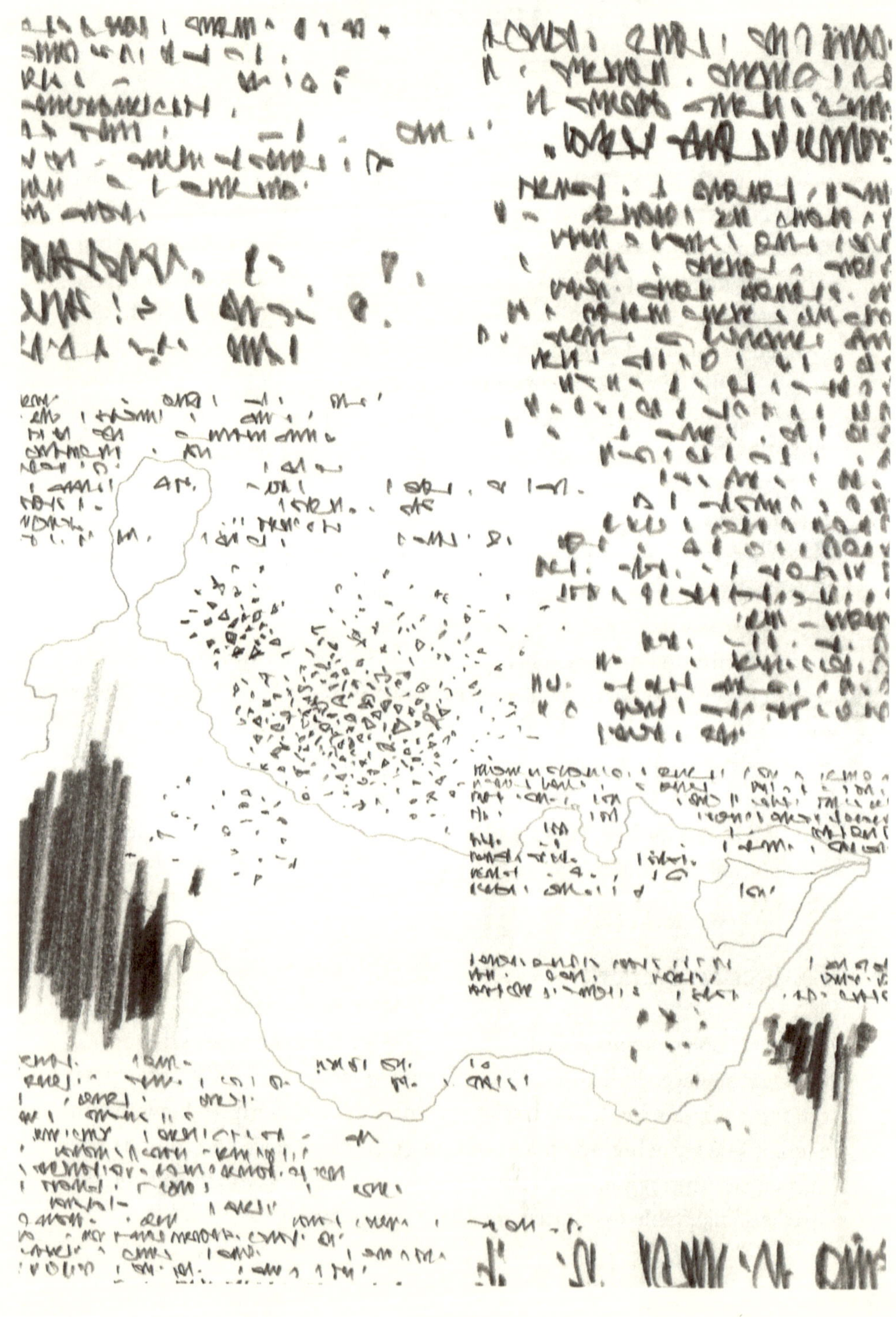

The Age of the Invertebrates

All life on Earth descended from LUCA, the 'last universal common ancestor'. This was not the first lifeform but was the most resilient, prolific, and notably the last before bifurcation led to all modern organisms. With this began the Age of Early Life during the Archean eon, 3.7 Ga ago. This was when Earth first awoke and began its climatic swings and geological supercontinent cycle, as it sought to extinguish life from its surface. This, it then timed, leading to a lethal combination of events that caused its first **mass extinction**.

This was the Precambrian and Vendian Mass Extinction, 650 Ma ago. The reset this caused pushed life to new limits. What survived quickly adapted, evolved into new, enhanced lifeforms that gained sufficient resilience to persist and then thrive. This rebirth led to the Cambrian Explosion of Life. This, what emerged, then ended the Precambrian supereon, along with the Age of Early Life, which dawned the present Phanerozoic eon, beginning the Age of Invertebrates with the Paleozoic era.

The primitive invertebrate life that had emerged was sufficiently resilient to persist through the ensuing climatic extremes. The first was the ninety-five-million-year-long Cryogenian Ice Age that transformed Earth into a snowball. At its end, it took 200 Ma for Earth to thaw, only to be followed by another, albeit shorter – the thirty-million-year-long Andean-Saharan ice age. Neither climatic event extinguished life; rather, each forced life to further evolve and change. From this, emerged vertebrates, who then faced the second most lethal event in Earth's history, being also the last climatic extinction event. This was the Ordovician-Silurian mass extinction 444 Ma ago. After this event, Earth's geological activity intensified, eventually climaxed to cause the next, the late Devonian mass extinction 378 Ma ago. Earth then froze for 71 Ma with the minor Karoo ice age before again, geological activity began to intensify, which then rifted the supercontinent Pangea apart. This then caused the Great Dying, Earth's most lethal near life-ending event. With this ended the Age of Invertebrates.

The Ages of Reptiles and Mammals

As the Age of Invertebrates ended, Earth began seething again. Its tantrums were causing the rifting of the supercontinent Pangea. Widespread volcanic activity with lava spews began covering the surface, causing climate change. This began the last greenhouse period that would last for 226.1 Ma, and as events peaked, this then caused the Great Dying, the Permian-Triassic mass extinction 252 Ma ago.

The Great Dying was caused by the Earth's supercontinent cycle, which had rifted Pangea apart. The tension this produced exploded with the intense volcanic outpouring of flood basalt, releasing gigantic pulses of carbon dioxide. As this continued for thousands of years, it eventually acidified all of Earth's oceans, extinguishing 96 per cent of all marine life. On land, this event decreased oxygen levels, caused acid rain, and increased global temperatures, producing hellish global warming. What survived abandoned the oxygen-deprived seas and became terrestrial. At its end emerged the oldest common terrestrial ancestors together with seeded plants and flying insects. From this, it then took a further 4 Ma years for the Age of Reptiles to begin.

From the aftermath of the Great Dying, Earth knew it had lost its fight; it could not extinguish life from its surface. What it had begun, however, could not be undone; the supercontinent cycle could not be halted or stopped. As the rifting process continued, it tore both Laurasia and Gondwanaland apart, which then caused the Triassic-Jurassic mass extinction 201 Ma ago. This event, however, did not lead to a reset as life had already become sufficiently resilient to endure Earth's tantrums. What then followed was beyond Earth's control and beyond lives' resilience to endure. A fifteen-kilometre-wide meteorite struck the Gulf of Mexico at the Yucatán Peninsula, opening a 180-kilometre-wide crater. A huge blast and heatwave followed that also threw huge amounts of debris into the air and caused massive tidal waves to wash over continents. This caused the Cretaceous-Paleogene mass extinction 66 Ma ago, an event that then ended the Age of Reptiles and ushered in the new Age of Mammals.

The Universal Beat

A pulse beat at creation. This was the big bang. This was the first heartbeat that set everything in motion. It then took hundreds of millions of years to pulse again, timed with what unfolded in this universe. This then set the standard that now governs everything – how galaxies, stars, and planets form and how life is to evolve on this plane. From this came the laws of vibration, rhythm, and constant motion and the law of perpetual transmutation of energy, tying and synchronising everything with the **pulse**.

Within this pulse exists a varying beat. This is the universal beat, which becomes evident as history is replayed in fast-forward. From this emerges a clear rhythm, marked by a synchrony of events. This can also be taken forward to provide glimpses at destiny, to reveal what is bound to occur.

This beat expands or contracts proportionate with scale, complexity, and size. The largest object known is this solar system, which takes 230 Ma to revolve once around its centre to complete one galactic year. This is then infinitely quickened as objects diminish. The next largest known is this planetary system, which takes 25,772 years to traverse through its zodiac and complete one equinoctial cycle, one great year. The Earth, being infinitely smaller again, beats faster with its years, seasons, months, days, and hours, all in part also influenced by its lunar cycle as it orbits around its sun.

Despite what seems well beyond comprehension, having apparent great complexity as to how things are ordered and then move, there is an overriding simplicity that defines these. Some may appear to be random anomalies or contradictions, like erratic pulsar stars with their rapid rotation, taking milliseconds to complete one cycle, but even these, with their varying beats, become understandable when considered tied and synchronised rhythmically with this universe's constant pulse.

The Great Acceleration of Life

The great acceleration of life began after Earth coalesced into existence, had sufficiently cooled, and gained its first, hydrogen-based atmosphere. Chemical reactions then ensued, producing RNA (ribonucleic acid) and DNA molecules. From this came simple cells – prokaryotes, which then provided the basis for all further life to manifest. This first and initial step had taken 1.78 Ga to complete, which then quickened with its next step, when multicellular life emerged 1 Ga later.

Evolution was progressively quickening, shortening each successive step. This enabled the first animals to emerge some 800 Ma ago. From this emerged the reptiles 480 Ma later, followed by the first mammals, 142 Ma later. Then came the first primates, 123 Ma later, followed by the hominins, 49 Ma later, and by the *Homo sapiens* 5.6 Ma later.

Each step was **evolutionary**. Each progressed life to a higher form. Each new lifeform then defined Earth's era, establishing its own age. The first, the Age of Early Life, was 2.9 Ga long. The next, the Age of Invertebrates (including the Ages of Fish and Amphibians) lasted 292 Ma. Next, the Age of Reptiles was shortened to 183 Ma, which then was followed by the present age, the Age of Mammals, being 65 Ma long.

Earth's evolutionary progress had started with an initial crawl that turned to a walk and now a sprint. What initially took billions of years had accelerated to hundreds of millions and then to tens of millions of years. This is how life on Earth progressed, accelerating to reach some end. This, however, has not stopped with us. We are only the present outcome of this acceleration.

The Great Acceleration of Geological Time

Events on Earth changed life as much as life then changed Earth.

As Earth tried to extinguish life, life fought back, forcing change on Earth to suit itself. This then set Earth's geological time, with its supereons, eons, eras, periods, and epochs, all defined by what occurred, what lived, what perished, and what fossilised.

The longest span of continuous geological time was also Earth's first and oldest age, known as the Precambrian supereon. This supereon was defined by Earth's earliest life, which also caused its end. Its end came when life gained form and became multicellular. From this then emerged and came everything since, all subsequent life.

Everything since happened during the significantly shorter present Phanerozoic eon. This is despite this eon having the three eras that progressed life at a quickening pace to produce all that exists today. The life that emerged at the start of each era also defined Earth's age, and from the first to the present, it also matched Earth's pace for change, persisting through its mass extinction resets. What eventuated was a quickening that shortened each subsequent era and **accelerated** evolution. This forced, hastened, and pushed life, which progressed, gained further resilience and complexity, and at times reached its ultimate form before either being consumed by Earth or devolved by time.

The first and oldest era is the Paleozoic. This era is also the longest at 292 Ma long. The second, the Mesozoic Era, is an age that was shortened from the previous by 109 Ma. The last is also the present, the Cenozoic era, which is likely to be further shortened to a fraction of all the previous ages. This shortening of geological time has quickened the rate and pace of evolutionary change, which inevitably is bound to soon accelerate past the human species.

The Quaternary Period

The present Cenozoic era has a readily apparent quickening. Within this geological age, life has rapidly evolved, progressed through shortened steps, and from this emerged this era's most dominant form, having since commenced its own age, the Age of Humans.

We are presently living in the 2.6 Ma long Quaternary period within the 65 Ma long Cenozoic era. Both seem eternal. However, compared to the vast spans of geological time, both are mere fractions of all that previously occurred.

The Quaternary period is the shortest in all of Earth's history. It is substantially shorter than its predecessor, the 63 Ma long Tertiary period. Equally, the recently ended Holocene epoch, being 11,628 years long, is a mere fraction of its predecessor, the 2.58 Ma long Pleistocene epoch.

As much as we became a product of the **quickening** that occurred, we have since taken control and become the cause and instigators of change. By our actions ending the Holocene epoch, we made this our age, the Anthropocene epoch, the Age of Humans.

What we have done, we are still doing, which has since accelerated the pace of change. We are the cause of the present looming global change. We have caused Earth's climate to wildly fluctuate, oscillating between its extremes. We have also taken many species to the brink of extinction.

With all our intellect and know-how, we should know better. We have the means to control what occurs, set our fate, and secure our future, but rather, we allow our self-centred nature to rule us. We focus on short-term wants, seeking to always improve our present condition and station while disregarding all that might eventuate.

With all the change we have caused thus far, we have increased the probability that a global reset will soon occur, and if this does, then our time as the dominant species on Earth, during this age, will likely end, as will the Quaternary period.

The Rise of Human Intelligence

Imagine if our species – the AMH, with its 315,000 years of evolution – was doubled or tripled or had a twenty - or thirty-fold increase. This is what the ancients had.

The ancients had lived on earth for 25 Ma. During the first 15 Ma, they struggled with the aftermath of the 252 Ma mass extinction reset. Eventually, they overcame adversity by harnessing their intellect and using this to dominate the landscape. The next 6.3 Ma years gifted them superior intellect with psionic abilities, which they progressively enhanced. It then took a further 3.1 Ma of refinement and experimentation for the ancients to gain the means to exit the cycle of life and become immortal. Such a long evolutionary time would change any species from its most primitive form to a super-intelligent godlike being.

We too are on the path towards **immortality**. We, however, have only recently begun our journey and need substantially more time to evolve past our present, relatively primitive state of being. The blessing is the quickening of time that is occurring will enable us to achieve what the ancients had in a shorter time. But, to realise our destiny, we must learn to be patient so we can peacefully endure and survive the time required for this to become reality. When or if this occurs, it will be our distant future descendants who will realise this. If they are fortunate, evolutionary time will also expand their minds, gift them greater awareness, superior intellect, and psionic abilities. This will then also gift them the means to transcend past their mortal state into some post-human form, and when this does occur, then everything we had achieved, thought, and known will pale into insignificance to what they become. This is the transformative evolutionary change that will gift humanity the means to exit from this cycle of life and become immortal.

The Rise of the Ancients Part 1

The ancients' direct ancestors had experienced Earth's most concerted and lethal attempt to extinguish life on its surface. This was the Great Dying. Extensive volcanic activity ensued as Pangea rifted apart. Temperatures oscillated between extremes, causing severe climate change. Earth's oceans acidified, and what fell to Earth was acid rain. This continued worldwide for sixty-one thousand years, and then it took a further 15 Ma for Earth's climate to normalise and for life to again thrive.

This forced reset had devastated life. It ended the Age of Invertebrates. What survived had to quickly adapt, become sufficiently resilient and intelligent so to persist. The life that eventually emerged had evolved, diverged, and gained its own unique and distinct form, which then began the Age of Reptiles.

The ancients' lineage was one of many that emerged from this forced reset. Physically, they were comparably weak, vulnerable, having a small, compact body, virtually powerless against the megafauna that existed. What they lacked in strength, however, they overcame with their superior intellect and later with psionic abilities.

The ancients were unlike any other species. They were highly intelligent, motivated, and had focused at attaining the highest gaols possible. After having lived on Earth for 6 Ma they began sensing that time and evolution would eventually devolve and end their lineage. They had also realised the Great Dying that had occurred 21 Ma before could reoccur. This then began their quest to attain immortality and find a means to exit from the cycle of life. They achieved this 3 Ma later when a **transcendence** occurred. This had gifted them the means to transform themselves, at will, into pure essence, energy, and intelligence. With this they then severed ties with mortal life, exited from the cycle of life, and became immortal. As ethereal beings, they gained form by occupying replaceable reptilian avatars. This then led to their eternal quest; to create an enhanced and eternal synthesised form.

The Sixth Dimension

Extraordinary things are possible with psionic abilities. When applied, the power unleashed can transform and reconfigure matter. When magnified, this then provides the means to dematerialise matter, including living beings. A transformation occurs that changes the complete molecular structure of matter, even a mortal form into energy and pure essence. In this form, travel anywhere becomes a reality, including out of existence and into higher dimensions.

The ancients achieved this, with their psionic abilities they had detached themselves from the third-dimensional realities and left all their limitations. This, they achieved through a merge, a formed collective that produced an enhanced community mind that magnified and focused their powers. This, they then used to exit from the cycle of life and migrate into the sixth dimension, the out-of-phase realm.

All who enter or what is taken into this realm are **transformed** by the pulsing resonance that exist there. This causes matter to alternate in and out of existence as it synchronises out of phase and disappears from the third dimension. For living beings, what occurs expands their minds' capacity, clearing access to all previous dormant areas, gifting some godlike abilities. The pure essence of intelligence has become part of this. It is there to realise its destiny having since become the one community mind that connects all within this realm.

When the third dimension is seen from the sixth, every conceivable place – together with all there ever was, is, and will be – becomes visible and accessible. This is so as both space and time have form and are malleable in this realm. This makes the impossible possible, allowing imagined realities to be brought into existence together with the rarest materials and machines that can then be placed anywhere in time and space.

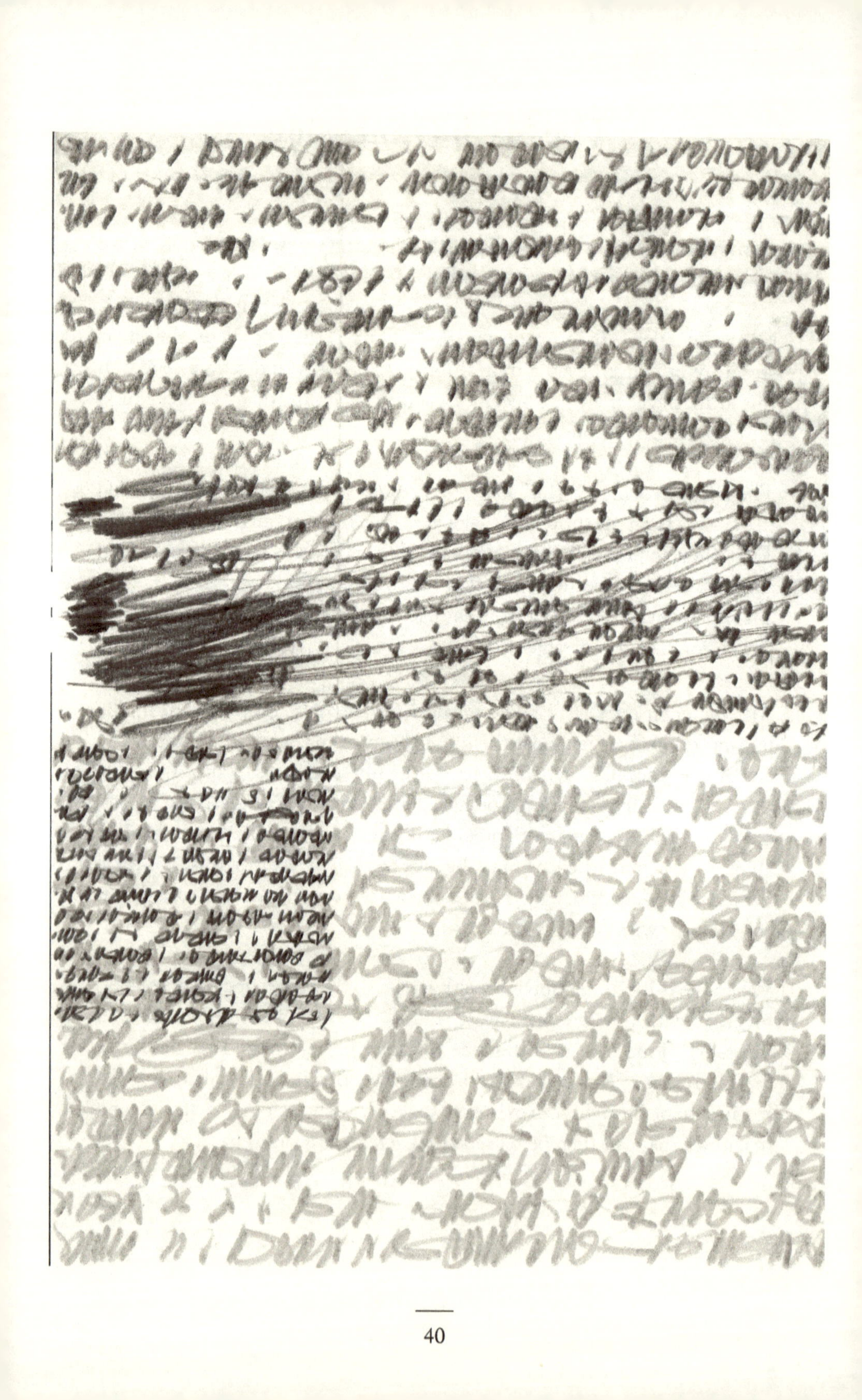

The Age of Mammals

Descendants from the first single-cell organism, LUCA, became bacteria, archaea, complex multicell organisms, and eventually all the life that now exists on Earth. Earth had facilitated this by forcing evolutionary change with its tantrums. The first notable tantrum caused the Precambrian and Vendian mass extinction. Seventy per cent of all lifeforms perished from this, but with this came a rebirth, a renewal, by way of the Cambrian Explosion of Life. What emerged replaced all that had previously existed with new enhanced, further evolved lifeforms. The Precambrian supereon ended as the Age of Invertebrates began. It had taken 3.2 Ga for LUCA to evolve into invertebrates, and as this occurred, it then also ended the longest evolutionary step in Earth's history.

This did not stop the resets that occurred, which continued, forcing invertebrates to become vertebrates and then fish, amphibians, reptiles, and finally mammals. This took 395 Ma to unfold, for invertebrates (sponges) to give form to the first mammal. What emerged was small,

insignificant,

nocturnal – an insect-feeding mammal that had to content with large prehistoric megafauna. Fate then intervened with the last mass extinction reset which ended the Age of Reptiles and provided mammals with clear pathways to dominate. As they began to thrive, this then began the Age of Mammals.

The meek shall inherit the Earth.

The rise of the mammals was, in part, facilitated by the ancients. They had begun experimenting and manipulating their ancestors, the stem mammals 227 Ma, who they forced to evolve so to gain a more enduring form. From the many variant forms that emerged, came one who became the most enduring, resilient, and intelligent lifeform: the AMH.

The Great Manipulation

How did we get here? Were we created? Was our evolution forced, assisted, or was it natural?

We are an outcome; we became because everything before us – all that preceded us, each of our ancestors – had the ability to persist through many life-ending events and resets. Possibly, the most enduring form that enabled this was the stem mammal. This early form of our ancestors had the resilience to endure both the Permian-Triassic and the Triassic-Jurassic mass extinctions.

The ancients' lineage had also survived the Great Dying, the first of these two-mass extinctions, but unlike the stem mammals, they then quickly evolved and attained an ultimate form. This had been their time as providence gifted them superior intellect with psionic abilities. This then enabled them to transcend past mortal existence and attain immortality. They achieved this by migrating to an out-of-phase realm that then shielded them from Earth's next tantrum, the Triassic-Jurassic mass extinction that occurred 201 Ma ago. The stem mammals, however, could not avoid this and had to endure this event, but from this, along with the ancients' manipulation, they transformed, and became true mammals. With this, our ancestors then gained a more enduring form, enabling them to survive what came next, the Cretaceous-Paleogene mass extinction.

From the ancients' out-of-phase realm, they foresaw how this would unfold on Earth. They admired the resilience of the stem mammals, along with their descendants. They assisted in its transition as they knew this was the lifeform destined to dominate the next era. Wanting access to the mammalian DNA, they then proceeded to manipulating its genetics so to ensure compatibility and quicken its evolutionary pace. They did this because they needed an assured source of replenishable and replacement DNA that they could use to upkeep their synthesised form. It however, took 49 Ma of genetic manipulation for stem mammals to become true mammals and another 123 Ma to produce the first primate. From this then came what the ancients had sought, the AMH, 54 Ma later.

The Emergence of the Modern Humans

The evolutionary journey of the AMH was achieved partly by design, combined with fate and chance. From the first common ancestor, LUCA to the first hominin, it had taken 3.77 Ga. It then took a further 6 Ma of forced evolutionary change for the first AMH to emerge. The ancients' manipulations had enabled this. They had fast-tracked evolutionary change through an introgressive hybridisation process that progressively blended genes and produced enhanced variant forms. This process bypassed millions of years of otherwise necessary evolutionary time.

When the AMHs first emerged 315,000 years ago, they were amid many rival, older-variant hominin forms. These first AMHs were vulnerable as they were still primitive and needed further time to evolve, mature, and gain intellect. Their nature, however – adventurous and promiscuous – gave them an immediate advantage. They ventured globally and were able to rapidly increase their tribal numbers, giving them the means to outcompete their rivals.

Behind the scenes, the ancients were helping the AMHs. They were progressively enhancing the genetics of certain AMH individuals, trialling their ability to attain **longevity**, superior intellect, and psionic abilities. The genetics that survived experimentation were then used to progress the AMH lineage. This continued until a form emerged that had comparable longevity, intellect, and psionic abilities as the ancients. This came 178 Ma after the ancients had first begun to manipulate the mammalian lifeform. This came with Adam, the most evolved and advanced human who ever lived.

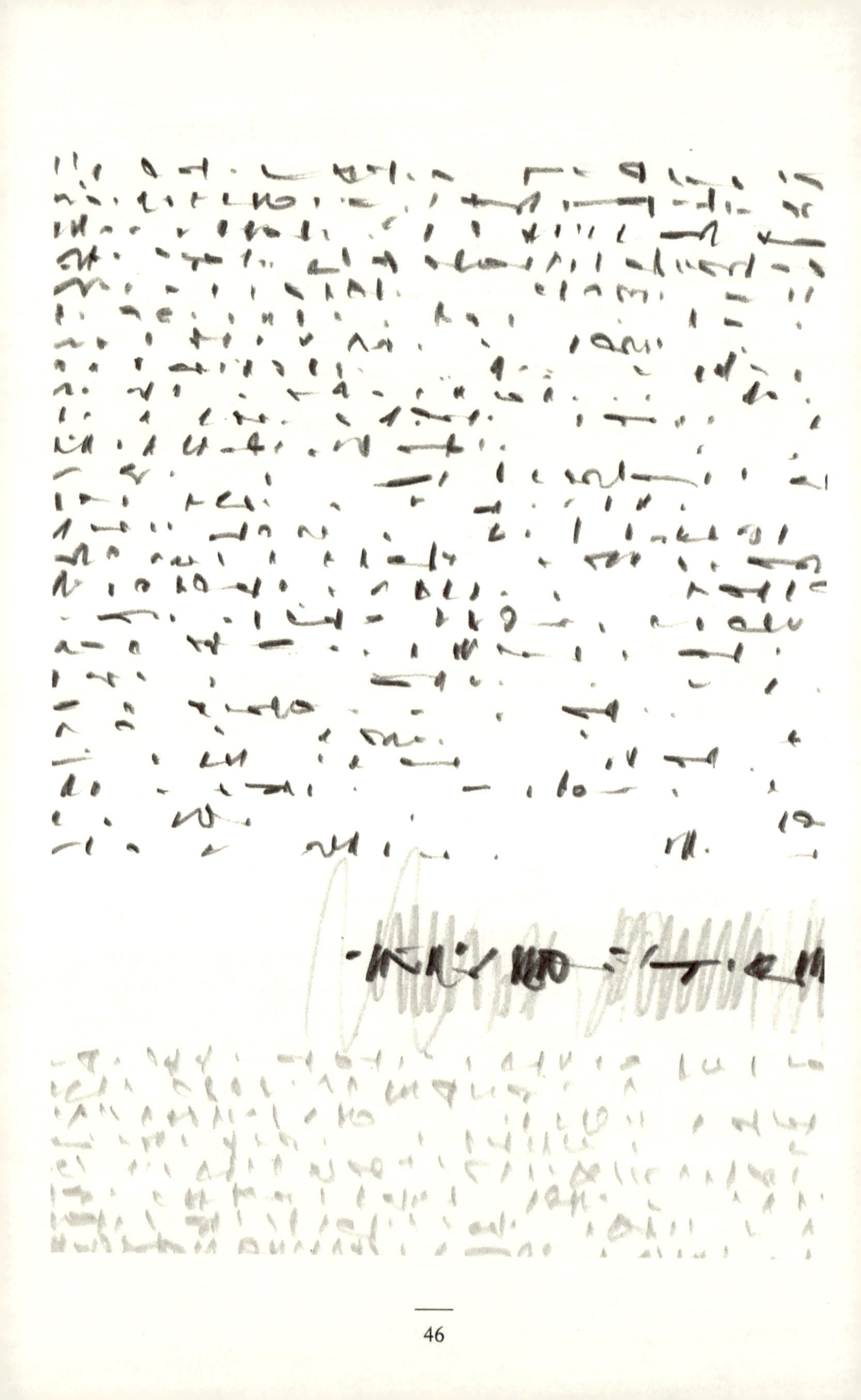

THE REPETITIVE CYCLE OF LIFE

All that is to occur, the likely future, can be foretold by peering back and seeing how the repetitive cycle of life had previously unfolded.

Earth's many mass extinction resets came by way of continental shifts, meteor strikes, and **prolonged** catastrophic climatic change that took and held temperatures at extremes. The life that endured these events then evolved to gain resilience so to persist until it could again thrive. This is the repetitive cycle of life. Simplified, life on Earth can be represented by a large tree, being the tree of life. Each branch represents a different type of life, sprouting to give form to each of its kin and descendants. Seasonal variations set the rhythm for all that occurs. When winter comes, some branches wither and die, and leaves are shed, and as the season turns to spring, new growth is enabled that brings forth rebirth with renewal. This is how life is progressed, from birth to maturity, where it is destined to cause a rebirth before its death. Lifeforms fortunate to persist and not perish are able to evolve further, gain resilience and maturity, and eventually transform to become a more enduring lifeform. This is what brought forth all the past realities with all the eras and ages, and this will take life forward to its destiny.

All the life that now exists had ancestors that survived all the previous mass extinctions and every turn of the cycle of life. This is what made us who we are and our lineage sufficiently resilient so to endure further such change and greater adversity. However, there are limits. There is a likelihood that a cascade of events could occur. One random event not considered likely, which is past due by 473,000 years, is Earth's pole reversal. When this occurs, it will temporarily remove Earth's geomagnetic shield and expose the surface to charged particles, solar winds, and cosmic rays. This would corrupt life, decimate crops, cause illness, and destroy our digital society. If combined with several other equally destructive events, these could cause our demise and would also end the present 2.58 Ma long Quaternary period.

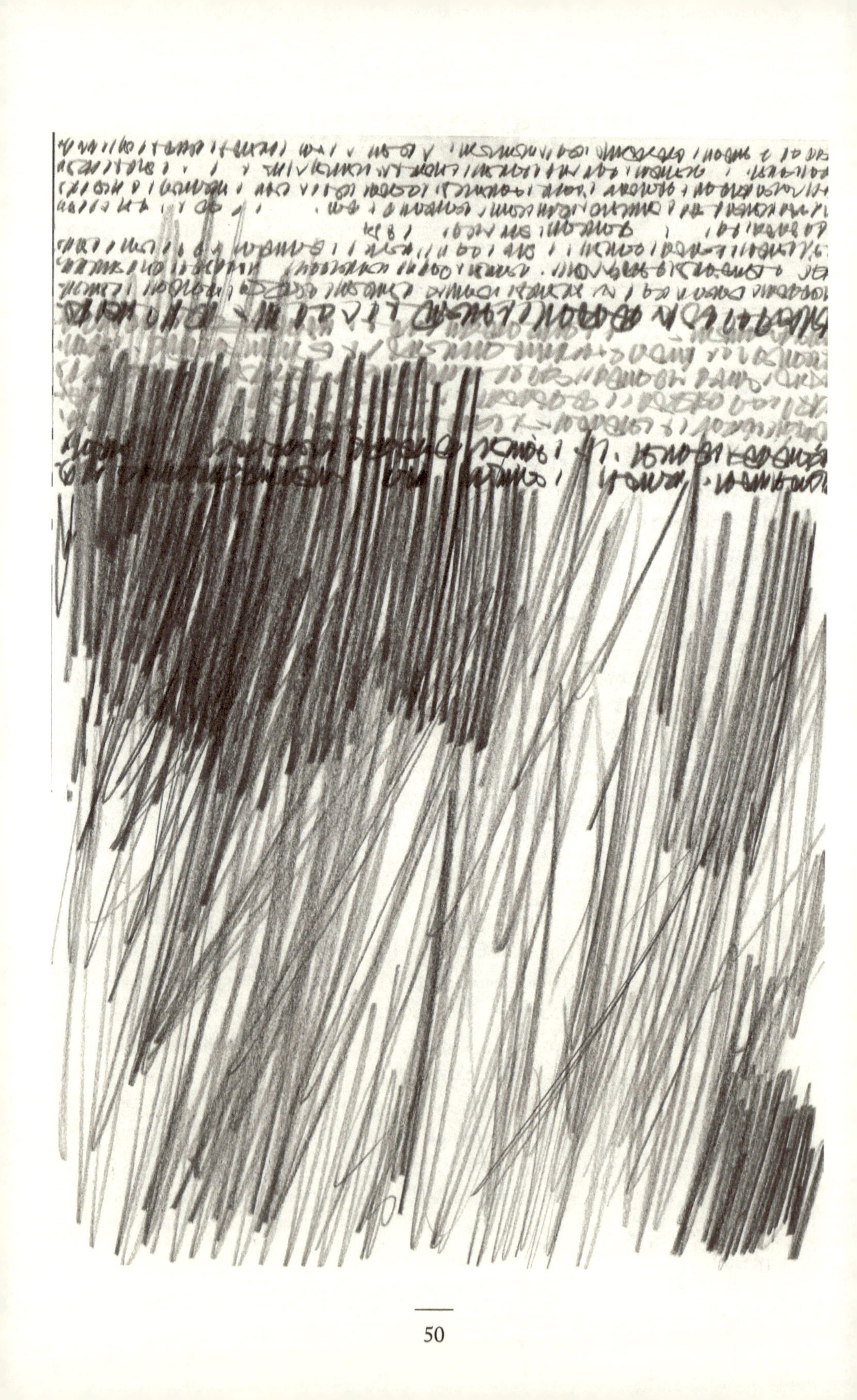

The Age of Early Life

Around 4.571 Ga ago, a supernova shock wave condensed a nearby gaseous cloud that caused our sun, with planets, to coalesce out of a solar nebula. What formed then moved erratically. Planets regularly crossed paths, which, 43 Ma later, led to the moon colliding with Earth. Both were then entrapped by each other's pull. It took another 40 Ma for their orbit to stabilise, which then brought 400 Ma of calm. Earth was still seething, molten, slowly cooling from this interaction when destiny interrupted with the Late Heavy Bombardment. For 300 Ma, the remnant matter from many destroyed and shattered worlds fell to Earth, depositing life forming material on its surface. This then awoke Earth.

Asteroids **deposited** colossal amounts of material on Earth's surface. This material eventually formed Earth's crust and oceans and enabled life to manifest. It then took 20 Ma for LUCA, the oldest known ancestor of all subsequent life, to appear. This then began lives' evolutionary journey on Earth, pushing life regularly to new limits so to progressively increase its complexity and resilience.

Earth's first atmosphere, being hydrogen based, began with a climatic greenhouse period that was the longest in Earth's history, lasting 1.7 Ga. When this ended 2.9 Ga ago, it began the 120 Ma Pongola glaciation, the first ice age that froze and transformed Earth. The sheer weight of miles-thick ice sheets that formed during this ice age led to plate subduction and formed Earth's first continental crust. The land that emerged then enabled single-celled organisms to evolve, becoming the first microbial life, which then began to photosynthesise.

As Earth established its continental crust and transformed itself, life also positioned itself so to create a habitable planet. Its photosynthesis process began to change Earth's atmosphere, which then inadvertently caused the first and necessary reset of life. This became the catalyst for all that was to come. This was the first mass extinction, caused by the Great Oxidation Event 2.4 Ga ago.

Lives' First Reset

Earth's atmosphere began to change 2.4 Ga ago as microbial life photosynthesised. This then caused the first mass extinction – lives' first reset. Oxygen was **lethal** to the anaerobic bacteria that then existed, which needed hydrogen to survive.

The photosynthesis process eventually oxygenated the atmosphere, which then lowered temperatures and took Earth's climate to its colder extreme. From this began the 300 Ma-long Huronian Glaciation, Earth's longest ice age. The extreme cold that ensued forced the oxygen-producing cyanobacteria to evolve further. Soon, this lifeform began to metabolise, transforming itself into plant life, albeit still microscopic. This then became the most evolved lifeform on Earth, and by having the ability to outgrow and outbreed all other lifeforms, it also proved to be the most resilient, which then enabled it to dominate the era.

The Great Oxidation Events

As much as Earth tried to change life, life then changed Earth.

The struggle for life to persist on the Earth's surface began 3 Ga ago, during the Archean eon. This was when Earth's plate tectonics had activated and begun its 500 -Ma-long supercontinent cycle. This was a process that forced Earth's continental crust to collide, forming supercontinents, only to then be rifted apart into smaller landmasses.

Life then began to influence what occurred on Earth. The first reset came with the Great Oxidation Event. This oxygenation affected Earth's atmosphere which led to the first ice age. At its end, Earth took its climate back to its natural state, and what followed was a 1.3 Ga long greenhouse period. This then ended with a repeat of what had previously occurred. Life intervened with its second oxygenation event, known as the NOE (Neoproterozoic Oxygenation Event). This then caused Earth to freeze again, beginning the 85 -Ma- long Cryogenian glaciation, the second ice age.

The extreme freezing that ensued turned Earth into a snowball. The global mean temperature dropped to 12°C below freezing. This then coincided with supercontinent cycle rifting activity that pushed life to new limits, causing the Precambrian and Vendian mass extinction, Earth's first attempt to extinguish life on its surface. This, with the extreme coldness of snowball Earth, extinguished 70 per cent of all lifeforms. What survived had to persist within the confines of thin, narrow equatorial strips, living in slush-covered icy ocean water.

Unbeknownst to both Earth and early life, this was a transformative event. This was the **catalyst** that forced life to further evolve and diversify. From this emerged the earliest animals: the trilobites, archeocyathids, and animal-like Caveasphaera, new resilient lifeforms that had adapted to Earth's fluctuating climate and conditions. With this, the Cambrian Explosion of Life occurred, which brought the Precambrian supereon to its end, 540 Ma ago.

The Cambrian Explosion of Life

After death and chaos come life and order.

The Precambrian supereon had provided suitable conditions for life to manifest and then evolve from single cells to complex **multicellular** life. The life that eventually emerged during this supereon could photosynthesise and metabolise. This early life had to contend with Earth's supercontinent cycle geological activity, which, at times, intensified, along with extremes in temperatures that took the climate from greenhouse periods to ice ages. As life persisted through such change and turmoil, it gained resilience and began to progress to higher, more complex forms. From this, simple single cells rapidly developed, adapted, and evolved. Natural selection ensured only the fittest and most resilient persisted. As life then evolved, it also began to transform. What then emerged caused the Cambrian Explosion of Life, which then ushered in a new age and the first era of the present eon. This was the Age of Invertebrates, the Paleozoic era of the Phanerozoic eon.

The Paleozoic era is the longest and the most turbulent of the Phanerozoic eon, being 292 Ma long. This is the era that endured the most change. It had three mass extinctions, three greenhouse periods, and two ice ages. The first mass extinction occurred during the 30 -Ma-long Andean-Saharan ice age. This was the Ordovician-Silurian mass extinction 444 Ma ago. The next, the late Devonian extinction, occurred 72 Ma later, during a 60 -Ma-long greenhouse period, the fourth in Earth's history.

From the first reset event emerged the Age of Fish and from the second the Age of Amphibians, all as part of the Age of Invertebrates. This era then ended during the last greenhouse period, when intensive supercontinent cycle rifting activity led to the Great Dying, the Permian-Triassic mass extinction 252 Ma ago. This was Earth's most concerted effort to extinguish life from its surface, being the most lethal event in all history. This then ended both the Age of Invertebrates and the Paleozoic era.

Continental Shifts

Once Earth coalesced into existence, it took near 100 Ma for its surface to sufficiently cool, solidify, and form its first, primordial crust. Then for 900 Ma, repeated destructive events caused Earth's crust to continually reform. Eventually, what emerged were the seven major tectonic plates that have since become the African, Antarctic, Eurasian, North American, South American, India-Australian, and Pacific continental plates, destined never to join. Extreme underlying pressure exerted by convection currents of slow-moving fluid, molten magma has kept these in constant motion, causing these to slide along, collide with, or rift from one another at 1.5 centimetres per year.

This began Earth's renewal cycle, its supercontinent cycle, a cycle that takes some 500 Ma to complete. With this formed the first supercontinent, Vaalbara, 3.6 Ga ago, followed by Ur 3 Ga ago and then Kenorland 2.5 Ga ago, Columbia 1.8 Ga ago, Rodinia 1.1 Ga ago, Pannotia 650 Ma ago, and finally Pangea 300 Ma ago. Once these had formed, the universal law of rhythm then took hold and proceeded to rift these supercontinents apart, dispersing and scattering parts worldwide, so this cycle could begin again.

The rifting of the last supercontinent, Pangea, caused the greatest impact on life. Tension between plates exploded with the intense volcanic outpouring of flood basalt that had effusively **erupted** in northern Pangea, at today's Siberian Traps. This released a volcanic spill-load the size of Australia, along with gigantic pulses of lethal carbon dioxide. This acidified Earth's oceans, the Panthalassa and Paleo-Tethys oceans, and led to intense global warming. Ninety-six per cent of all marine and 75 per cent of all land species perished. This was the single worst life-ending event. This was the Great Dying. What survived left the oceans as amphibians and became reptiles. The reset this caused then began a new era and the Age of Reptiles. From this emerged new distinct reptilian species, destined to rule Earth.

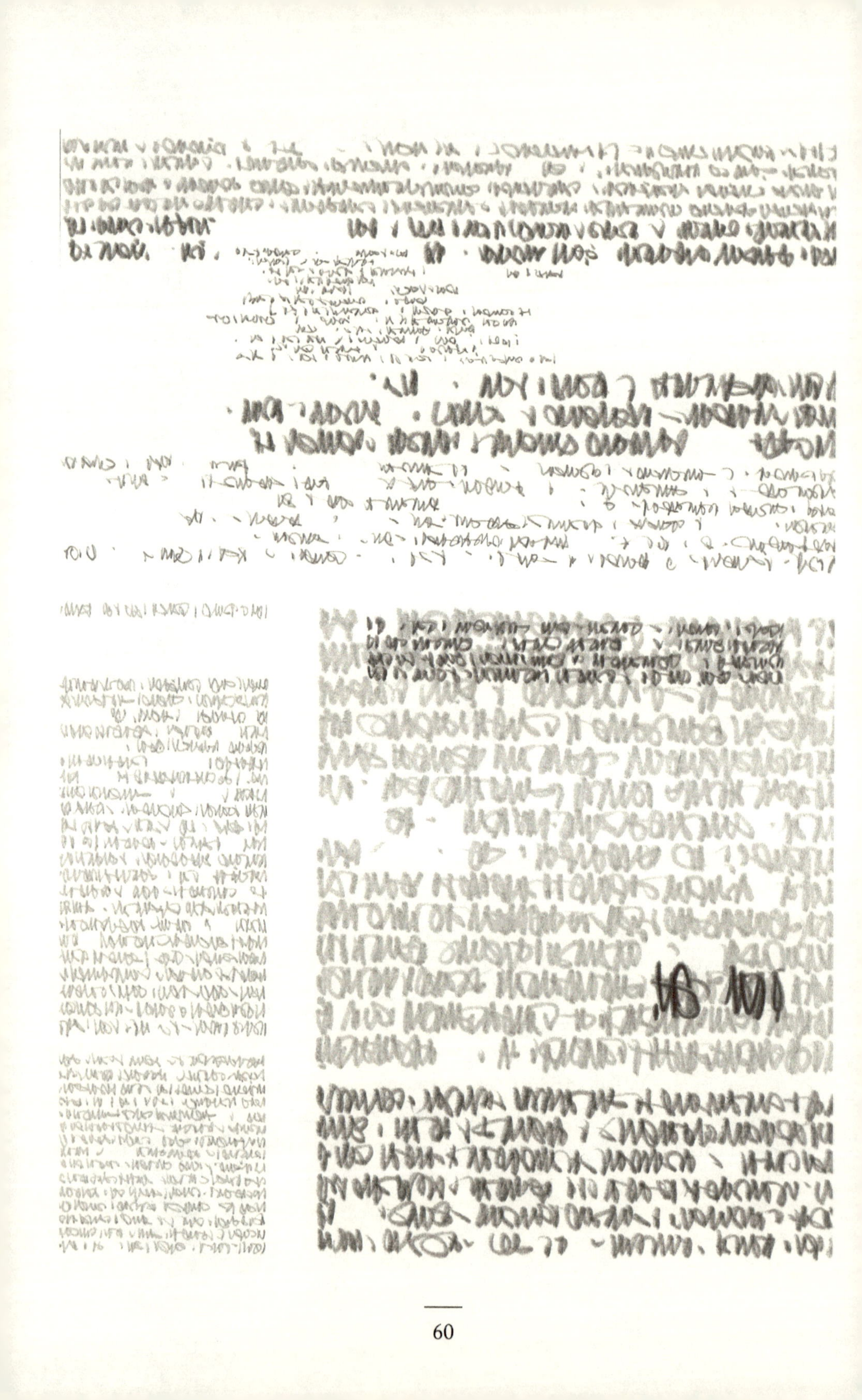

Continental Rifting to Present and Amasia

The process that rifted Pangea to Laurasia and Gondwanaland did not end with the Great Dying. This continued. It could not be halted or stopped as it was part of Earth's renewal cycle. This then climaxed again 51 Ma later, causing the next mass extinction: the Triassic-Jurassic extinction. Volcanic eruptions outpoured effusively intense flood basalt that again acidified the Earth's oceans and caused severe climate change. The mortality rate from this mass extinction, however, was reduced to 76 per cent.

Life had already learnt and became sufficiently resilient so to persist through such events. What survived then had the freedom to evolve further and became more enduring and resilient. This had enabled stem mammals to evolve and become the earliest true mammals.

As much as rifting reconfigured Earth's continents, so were its oceans. Oceans, however, need double the time to complete the superocean cycle. This occurs as oceans are recycled through alternating introversion and extroversion processes. One retains, and the other renews. As the rifting process turns supercontinents inside out, Earth then swallows its superocean, dragging the rifting continental crust around the globe to form a new middle, where either the old is recycled or a new superocean emerges that then surrounds the new supercontinent.

The last superocean, Panthalassa, having formed 700 Ma ago, is presently being recycled. Once, this ocean surrounded Pangea and covered 70 per cent of Earth's surface. Today the Pacific Ocean is all that remains, which is destined to disappear when the next supercontinent, aptly already named **Amasia**, emerges some 300 Ma from now. With this, as lands, seas, ecosystems, and environments are all merged, a vastly different reality will unfold. Everything then will change, including humans, and what emerges from the renewal will then bring forth its own new era and age.

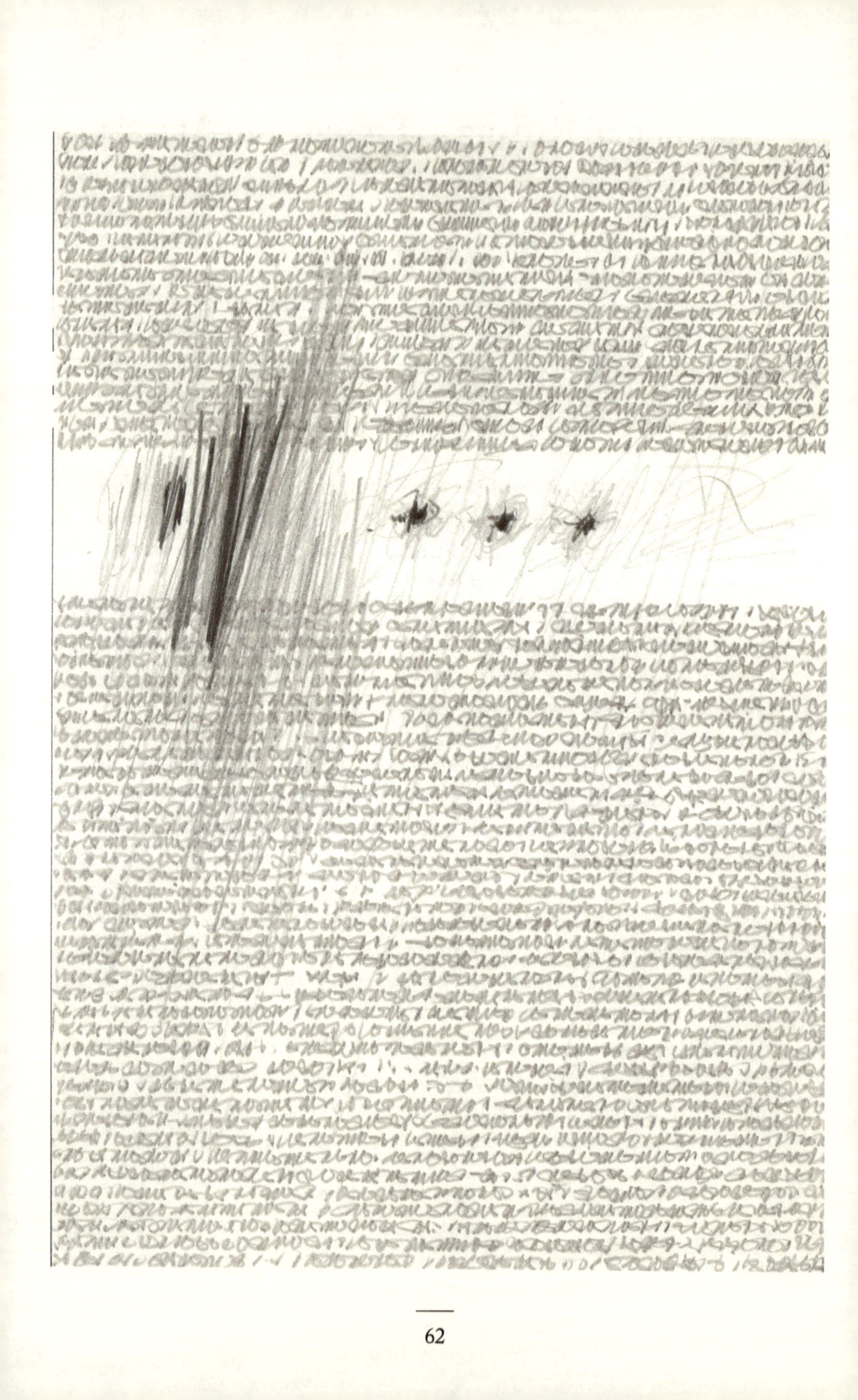

The Hot Earth

Throughout Earth's history, its climate has predominantly been in a greenhouse state. This is its natural state, having remained so for 85 per cent of all time. When change does occur, the climate then oscillates to its colder extreme, which commences an ice age. This climate fluctuation, from its greenhouse state to its colder extreme, has only occurred five times in Earth's history.

Earth's last **greenhouse** period began 260 Ma ago and lasted 226.1 Ma. This ended 33.9 Ma ago, when the present Late Cenozoic Ice Age began.

Earth's last greenhouse period proved ideal for all cold-blooded lifeforms. Both reptiles and dinosaurs thrived with the elevated temperatures. Winter in the polar regions ranged from 10°C to 25°C in summer. Palm tree forests grew on Antarctica's coastal lowlands and conifers with beech trees inland.

The last three mass extinctions occurred during this last greenhouse period. Each event added substantial greenhouse gases that fuelled global warming and kept temperatures high, on average at 30°C (86°F). When change came, it then took tens of millions of years for Earth's carbon cycle to absorb these gases.

The last mass extinction differed, however, as this was caused by an asteroid that struck earth 66 Ma ago. The debris thrown into the atmosphere initially dropped temperatures to their lowest known extreme. As this halted photosynthesis and froze the Earth, it also took life to new limits. All that previously dominated perished. Only the most insignificant and the smallest species were able to persist. What survived had to then rapidly adapt and evolve in new and different directions. The reset this event caused ended the reign of reptiles and dinosaurs on Earth. At the end of this initial freeze, global temperatures then jumped and stayed at 30°C for 10 Ma. This was Earth's hottest extreme for 474 Ma, since Precambria times. Despite hellish conditions, from this emerged the earliest and first primates, 21 Ma before the start of the present Late Cenozoic Ice Age.

The Asteroid Strike

After the second last mass extinction, life had 135 Ma of relative calm before the next and last: the Cretaceous-Paleogene extinction 66 Ma ago. This occurred when a fifteen-kilometre-wide asteroid struck Chicxulub, Mexico, causing a near life-ending explosion. This caused a reset that profoundly affected all life on Earth.

The death that ensued ended the Mesozoic Era, along with the Age of Reptiles. Species that survived had to adapt quickly and were forced to evolve along a different path. With this, the new life that emerged began the Age of Mammals.

The ancients had foreseen this event. They knew an asteroid would strike Earth and the dominance of the reptiles and dinosaurs would end. They were, however, powerless to stop or prevent this. All they could do was watch what occurred.

They **witnessed** the end of the Age of Reptiles. They also saw what survived and had previously dominated then devolve into prey. The ancients then knew they needed to find alternatives to their reptilian genetic sources. They had already begun manipulating the recently evolved mammals. Through an introgressive hybridisation process, a range of variant hybrid forms emerged, which were then blended to produce a more resilient and dominant form. This process bypassed millions of years of otherwise necessary evolutionary time.

Eventually, from this, the first primate emerged 55 Ma ago. This then set the new baseline for what was to come next, the numerous hybrid variant hominid lifeforms. With each, the ancients ensured they contributed to the introgression process, which progressed this lineage to hominins. This introgression process then ended 40,000 years ago, when the AMH became the sole remaining hominin survivor from this manipulated process. With this, the AMH had proven their worth to the ancients.

The Cenozoic Ice Age

Earth is presently in the Late Cenozoic Ice Age. This age began as temperatures plunged and ice sheets began forming in the polar regions 33.9 Ma ago. The climatic change from the last greenhouse forced life to quickly adapt so to persist with lower and colder temperatures. Forested landscapes became savannas, and mammalian lifeform diversified; some gained substantial body mass so to overcome the bitter cold. Then when the present Quaternary period began 2.58 Ma ago, Earth's Milankovitch cycle, its axial tilt and orbital eccentricity, began to vary, causing the climate to oscillate between glacial and interglacial periods.

Temperatures plunged when **the last glacial period** began 115,000 years ago. This advanced polar ice sheets into the middle latitudes of the Northern Hemisphere and lowered sea levels by more than 120 metres below present levels. This sea level drop opened land corridors with pathways to all continents, enabling the AMH to migrate out of Africa and reach every continent. They walked across the dry Mediterranean Basin into Europe. They then traversed on ice sheets from Asia to reach North America and walked on the risen Isthmus of Panama to reach South America. The last glacial period then ended as temperatures warmed, and the present warmer interglacial period began 11,700 years ago. The thawed ice then raised sea levels and again, the seas landlocked continents. With warmer temperatures, a new time began on Earth, the start the Holocene epoch.

The Present

During the present 2.6 Ma Quaternary geological period, Earth's climate has cyclically oscillated from its colder glacial maximum, which is set at 100,000 years long, to a warmer **interglacial** minimum climate, set at 15,000 years long. Recently, however, human-induced climate change has interfered with this cycle. This is likely to extend the present 11,700-year-long interglacial minimum by further hundreds of thousands of years and even has the potential to commence Earth's next greenhouse period.

Humans have contributed to all the change that now occurs. This began with the Neolithic Revolution, albeit having negligible effects, but has since expanded and accelerated, causing progressive change to all of Earth's atmospheric, geologic, hydrologic, and biospheric systems.

Our actions have devolved previous diverse landscapes, transforming these into monocultures and wastelands. We over-hunt, over-fish, spread pestilence, germs, and viruses, and introduce feral species that outcompete and then decimate native fauna. Rather than pause or halt the progressive change we do to Earth's systems, we have hastened our pace, leading to more damage as more of us are brought into existence.

In the last 500 years, our actions have extinguished 80 of the 5,570 mammal species and critically endangered many more. On this path, the irreparable ecological damage continues while a mass extinction looms. The forced renewal that is likely to occur threatens a reset that will end the Quaternary period, and if this causes our demise, then the Cenozoic era will also end. Species already at the brink of extinction will devolve to nothingness, while the most underestimated and insignificant, being insects, will likely emerge to dominate and begin their own era and age.

THE STORY OF THE ANCIENTS

The ancients' lineage emerged as a distinct species after the Great Dying. They lacked size and strength, and yet they thrived. Being relatively small, they had an abundance of speed, agility, and intelligence that made them a fierce competitor.

These ancients were prehistoric reptiles. They were unlike humans, having no hands, and thereby could not physically manipulate matter. They, however, had the ability to do extraordinary things with their minds, which eventually evolved to become psionic abilities. This then enabled them to **manipulate** space, time, matter, and all there was. With their psionic abilities, they had gained godlike powers, which they continued to refine and enhance until they gained the means to manipulate and create life itself.

The ancients had applied their gifted psionic abilities while knowing their time was limited. After their 22 Ma of existence on Earth, their genetics had begun to devolve. Their bodies had shrunk as they had no use for strength, muscle, or limbs, while their minds expanded and nearly outgrew their form. This forced them to find ways to transcend their mortal form and free themselves from Earth's hold. Through genetic manipulations, they experimented and began to produce many variant forms, including some of the fiercest dinosaurs. This, they then used to upgrade themselves, their form, so not to devolve further.

With their psionic abilities, they eventually found the key that enabled them to exit from Earth's cycle of life. They achieved this when they entered the out-of-phase realm. Freed from Earth's hold, they were able to further enhance and develop their genetic manipulation techniques, which eventually enabled them to synthesise their bodies. This led to a transcendence of their existence as they became immortals.

The Ancients' Out-of-Phase Realm

The sixth dimension is not easily or readily definable. Simply put, it is an out-of-phase realm that is well beyond our present perception and comprehension. Our governed minds are incapable of fully understanding, knowing, or appreciating this realm, and yet we are inextricably linked to it. It is also inexplicable how matter can be moved and transferred from the third to the sixth dimension. A transference occurs that rephases and reconfigures the molecular structure of the lesser dimensional matter. A sort of replication also occurs that reconstitutes the physical form of matter so it can exist in the fourth dimension. Physical beings with psionic abilities can, at will, re-phase themselves so to enter and reside within the fourth dimension.

As much as the third-dimension envelopes the first and second, so does each higher-level envelop their lower counterparts. And as much as the first and second are connected to the third, so does everything connect to their higher dimension. A congruency exists which links and ties the borders of all these dimensions. At such borders, when viewed from higher dimensions, they appear to expand well beyond, into the infinite, as compared with its lower dimension counterparts. From this border, when peering to the lower dimensions, everything appears finite and becomes visible.

From the higher dimensions, an apparent one-way **transparency** exists at the border locations with lower dimensions. This makes everything visible and accessible in the lower-dimensions. From the sixth and seventh, the structures of space, time, and matter appear fluid, in constant motion, like streaming water moving through the vacuum of space. Each is within reach and can be manipulated and altered at will. Time can be rewound or quickened, space folded back on itself, and matter reconfigured to produce new realities. Everywhere within this universe or adjoining multiverses, can be reached, seen, and experienced. With this, the ancients know all there ever was, all there is, and all that is likely to occur.

The Form of Pure Intelligence

Q is the architect of the out-of-phase realm. Q had created this realm and then phased it out of existence so it would not to be influenced by space or time.

This realm is an anomaly. It should not exist, but it does. Equally, what exists within this realm defies explanation and contradicts all known physical laws. This is the alternate reality that has made the impossible possible.

The **altered** reality created by this realm has enabled pure intelligence to gain form and substance and manifest into existence. This has become the one community mind that has since enhanced this realm by reconfiguring it so to enable a connected community of three, four and five-dimensional beings to exist within its boundaries, outside time and space, within the sixth dimension.

Pure intelligence has only one simple motive. It seeks to fulfil its destiny by finding and then merging with lost parts of itself. It seeks to re-join with all the forms of intelligence that the big bang has spread throughout this universe.

Those who reside within the realm interact through a complex tiered structure, like ants and bees, albeit in more sophisticated ways. Movement is through complex connected architecture of community spaces that constantly change to suit the occupying lifeforms. Species with psionic abilities are free to move – but not so the others. These others are the lifeforms that are experimented on. Some, who reside permanently within the realm are the failed experiments or morphed species that have no other home. They have since become servants, tasked with the maintenance and upkeep of this realm.

The one community mind monitors everything within the realm. It also disseminates pertinent thoughts, experiences, and knowledge that are relevant to each community. This, it does by a mind merge, which, at the the same time, harnesses the unused psionic power. This power, it then wields to keep the realm whole, together, and intact. This ensures this altered state does not implode back into the third dimension.

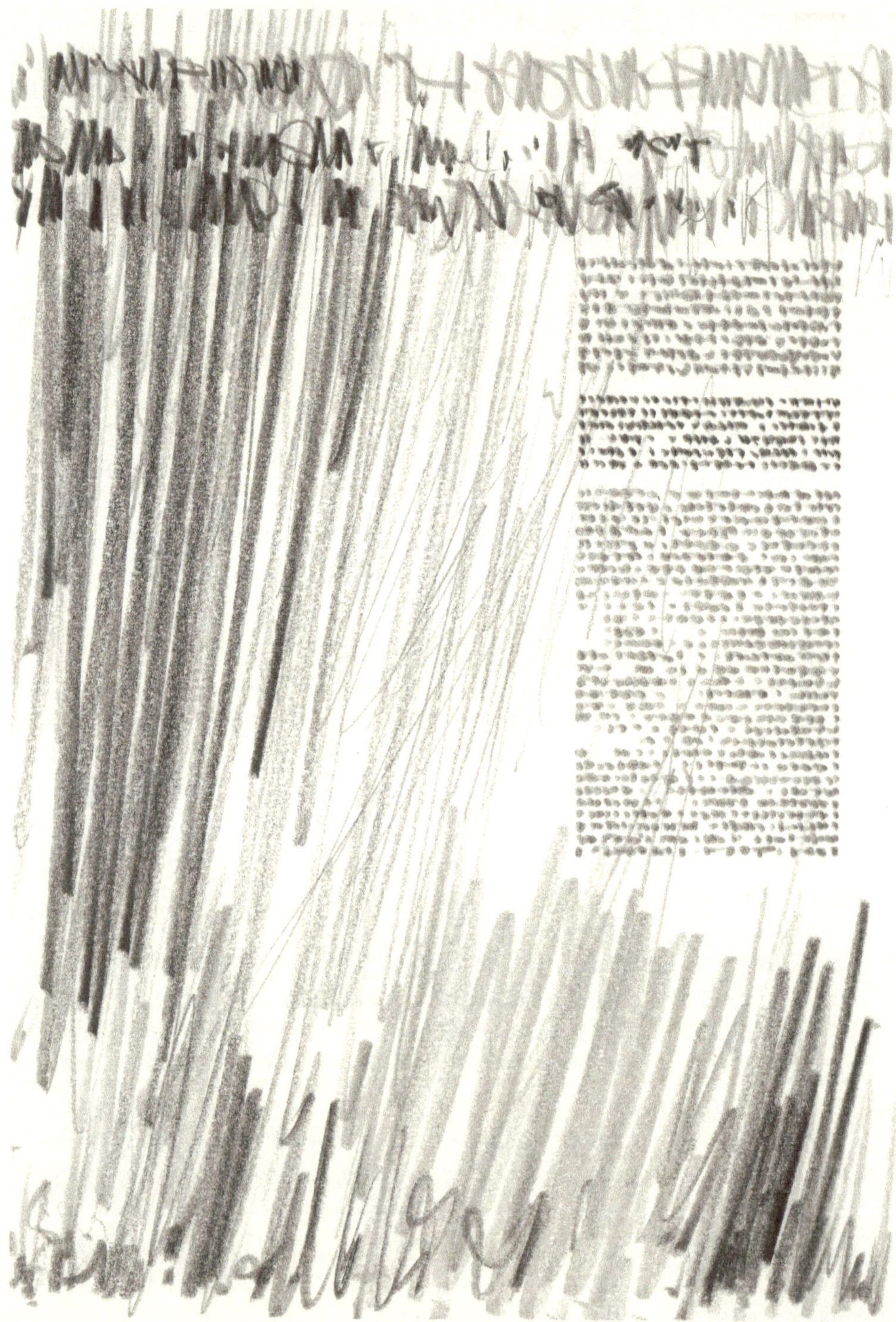

The One Community Mind

Benevolence and harmony reign supreme in the out-of-phase realm. Q's pervasive psionic abilities – along with the one community mind keep this realm intact. What they do, the power they harness and wield has enabled three, four and five-dimensional beings to exist within the sixth dimension – a miracle in itself.

Upon entry to this realm, the one community mind automatically connects, links, and merges with each new mind, scanning thoughts, abilities, and memories, ultimately to safeguard this realm. It also retrieves new knowledge which it then shares with the collective. As it does this, it also continually harnesses unused psionic powers, redistributing these with a resonance of feedback loops that enhances and magnifies the innate abilities and powers of each individual and the collective.

The magnitude of the power the one community mind can wield depend on how many minds with **psionic** abilities it has merged with. With what it can harness from the collective, it can already do otherwise impossible things. The power it has can bring into existence new realities, worlds, and creations. This however, is rarely utilised as everyone in the realm has already everything they need.

The one community mind is the true master of this realm. It is however a benign entity that waits to re-join with the scattered parts of itself and the original, the one omnipresent creator entity. This is its only quest, to be whole again. However, when this final merge does occur, it will then also bring this universe, with its reality, to its end.

The Rise of the Ancients Part 2

The Great Dying, which occurred 252 Ma ago, was followed by 15 Ma of extreme misery and turmoil. The life that managed to survive persisted by adapting to circumstances, changing, and diversifying so to gain resilience and an evolved form. From this forced reset emerged many new, distinct, and enhanced reptiles and dinosaur species. Some became the fiercest and largest megafauna, while others gained special abilities, intellect with reasoning. The ancients were so gifted with such abilities. This had made them superior to all other species, which enabled them to persist and then thrive.

At first, the ancients used their abilities to protect themselves from the **fiercest megafauna**. Soon, they began to dominate and later rule the lands. With their abilities, for a time, they established a sustainable balance on Earth among all species. Time then progressively changed and enhanced them. Eventually, they gained psionic abilities, which enabled them to control their destiny. They then had no need for protection, technology, or strength.

From their interactions soon emerged a community mind that connected all their thoughts, enhanced, and focused their abilities. As they experimented with this, they soon found they could manipulate space, time, and matter. 229 Ma ago, they gained the means to enhance their form and thereby stop the degrative devolution that had begun to corrupt their DNA. 2 Ma later, they gained the means to traverse into the sixth dimension and thereby exited the cycle of life, leaving behind their doomed dinosaur lineage. A further 1 Ma was required to synthesize and transcend their mortal form, and gain immortality.

The Ancients' Lineage and Dilemma

The ancients' earthly reptilian lineage has long been extinct. The DNA of what remained of them had completely corrupted. It had reached its end and could no longer evolve. However, long before this occurred, the ancients found the permanent solution of immortality.

Initially, to persist while their DNA devolved, they needed to maintain their form, which led them to enhance themselves with compatible genetics. This provided them with the time they needed to search, find an exit to the cycle of life and Earth. They achieved this when they found the key to the out-of-phase realm, the sixth dimension.

This presented them with limitless possibilities, enabling them to further manipulate their genetics. The gained the means to reengineer every atom and cell, redesign these so each would resonate in tune with their minds. This enhanced and expanded their minds, giving them the know-how and means to transform themselves fully and occupy synthesised bodies. By achieving this, the ancients became immortals.

As immortals, the ancients now contemplate all there was, is, and will be so to become all knowable and understand the **incomprehensible**.

With their enhanced abilities and powers, they can do all they want, including what is seemingly impossible. If they wish, they can move mountains, travel anywhere and everywhere, explore multiverses, or create new realities. This, however, they have already done and achieved. All they must do is continue to maintain their synthesised bodies while the search for an eternal form. This, they do while also contemplating and waiting for the next merge, when the one community mind will finally link with the original part of itself, the one omnipresent entity that created this universe and reality.

The Ancients' Manipulations

The ancients are different in every aspect from humans. They descended from a prehistoric reptile-dinosaur lineage that predated the emergence of the first mammal. Evolution and time then gifted them superior intellect with psionic abilities.

The ancients' quest began 229 Ma ago as they sought to upgrade their mortal form and gain immortality. This was when their minds began to expand and outgrow their physical form. Eventually, they found ways to upgrade themselves with reptilian enhanced DNA.

Upon entry to the out-of-phase realm, the ancients foresaw the likely future with the destined demise of their reptilian-dinosaur lineage. This spurred them to find a more enduring, resilient, suitable, and compatible form. This began their experimentations and manipulations on emerging species, one of which was the stem mammal. By their facilitating and then directing the evolutionary progress, eventually, the first mammals emerged, which were then followed by primates, the body form the ancients had sought. The ancients then doubled their efforts and hasten the evolutionary progress.

From this, emerged hominins, who were then progressively upgraded until they gained awareness with intellect. From this then emerged the AMH, the form that had the DNA the ancients had sought and would use to produce their enhanced synthesised form. With this began their transformation, both physically and biologically, eventually enabling the ancients to gain a humanoid mammalian form.

Transformed, the ancients now watch from the sixth dimension and, at times, intervene so to **guide** our progress.

What the ancients have done in the past to our ancestors, they are still doing to other species. We are only one of the many outcomes of their manipulations. They however, still also need us. Our bodies hold the DNA they still use to maintain their synthesised form. This, we are yet to acknowledge or accept as it is well beyond comprehension. And when we do finally accept this, we will then need an eternity of time to reconcile all that the ancients have done to us.

Time Manipulation

The universal pulse is felt as an alternating beat within the sixth dimension. Unlike the time rigidity of the third dimension, this can be manipulated and altered. It can be rewound or sped up, taken back to the past or to the distant future.

Time manipulation has enabled the ancients to experience Earth's origins and see its likely future. The future, however, is unlike the past as not all events are **permanent** or fixed. Most events are in constant flux, waiting for time to set these. Change is thereby possible as fate and chance are not entirely mutually exclusive. The only permanency is what destiny and providence has fated. Not even the ripples that cause time to dilate or random incidents can change destiny. What has been fated, providence has set and fixed. This is what rules life in this universe as this is what has decreed the fate of species and planets.

The ancients knew this was destined to happen, as they had foreseen this; the two last mass extinctions, and knew they could neither intervene nor change what was ordained to occur. Nothing could be done to prevent these as these were fixed events that were tied to the fabric of time and space. Changing these would have caused a large rift and rip in space, which would sever ties between realms, adjoining multiverses, and possibly cause this universe to implode.

The ancients nevertheless, found knowing what was destined to happen provided them with useful insight. They use this to prepare and expand their understanding and awareness of all that is and will be.

The Greater Consciousness

All that remains of the ancients' mortal existence is their essence, combined energy with intelligence. This, what remains, is their most valued, treasured asset, housed within each of their synthesised bodies.

The ancients' synthesised form has been technically designed. Each molecule has an imprint of their essence and intelligence, linked directly to a synthesised mind. Each molecule has also been configured, tuned, and aligned so to resonate, enhance, and magnify the mind's psionic abilities. With this, they can access every conceivable place and time, including the quantum world. There, they have found and tapped into an inexhaustible quantum power source. This has given them the means to transmit matter and thought messages anywhere, to any time and place in history. This quantum power with molecular transfer ability, not impeded by time or distance, has enabled the ancients to link their minds permanently with the one community mind that resides in their out-of-phase realm.

This is the ancients' merge with the one eternal entity of intelligence, an internet of sorts that gives them access to its vast reservoir of knowledge and experiences. With this merge, a mind transcendence has also occurred that dispelled their mortal wants and desires while enlightening with them with all there ever was, is, and will be.

This is what had enabled the ancients to realise their destiny. This is what had given the ancients the means to synthesise their bodies and overcome all their earthly **vulnerabilities**.

The ancients have no need or desire for comfort, and nor do they have emotions or wants. All of their mortal needs and wants were absorbed, overcome, or dispelled by this merge, when they integrated their minds and thoughts with the greater consciousness.

The Coming of a New Age

Life on Earth took 3 Ma to secure a firm foothold after the last mass extinction. At its end, this event decimated the ancients' source of suitable, harvestable reptilian-dinosaur DNA.

The ancients however, had already started their search for new sources, establish many new lifeforms with suitable, compatible, and enduring DNA. They had searched extensively throughout this universe and adjoining multiverses, travelling to all known habitable worlds. As they ventured, they spread their reptilian seed and DNA so to ensure future compatibility.

The ancients had foreseen that climate change would soon bring an ice age. This, they knew, would exacerbate their dilemma as their synthesised form, being **cold-blooded**, was reliant on species that were unable to generate sufficient internal heat or combat the extreme or prolonged coldness of an ice age. With this, the ancients also foresaw the rise and dominance of a new species, yet to emerge, which would persist, endure, and then thrive through the coming ice age.

To create such resilient enduring new species and ensure their compatibility, the ancients experimented on and manipulated the genetics of many species, which produced many hybrids and variant versions. Natural selection then tested each of these, culling most so what remained could evolve further. From this, emerged mammals, from which then came hominins and the AMH.

The ancients had facilitated this. They had fast-tracked the evolutionary process of our lineage with their periodic upgrades that instilled resilience and intelligence. This forced evolution was to establish a compatible and readily available supply of suitable mammalian DNA, which the ancients could use to create and then upkeep their synthesised form.

This is the awful truth and our predicament. It is our past and present, and is destined to be our future.

The Ancients' Eden

The sixth dimension is an unimaginable place. It is different in all respects to the third dimension. Its alternate reality is where the finite and the impossible have become the infinite and the possible. This is the ancients' Shangri-La. It is where they first took stem mammals to manipulate and experiment, and there emerged the first mammalian lifeform and then, hundreds of millions of years later, the biblical Adam and Eve. They were not the first modern humans but the most modern and evolved.

When Adam was created in Eden, he did not emerge in a nursery or sanctuary but in the ancients' laboratory. As the key outcome of the ancients' experiment, he was released so he could venture on Earth, tasked with setting the course for humans on Earth.

The sixth dimension is largely invisible to life living in the third dimension as it requires the third eye, psionic abilities to visualise it. This is thereby the place where only the most evolved beings, having psionic abilities, reside. Lesser beings without psionic abilities are either taken there or created within this realm. They can, however, freely exit from this realm but first need to find the return key: the will and want to leave. This is how Adam and Eve left Eden. With their **willpower**, they opened a portal that led to Earth, a place they would see and experience for the first time. As they entered the portal, they traversed trillions of light-years in milliseconds, placing themselves instantly at their destination.

Their exit from Eden was not stopped by the ancients as they were the outcome of the manipulations of the mammalian lifeform. This was pre-planned, so Adam and Eve would populate Earth.

The Last Glacial Maximum

The present Late Cenozoic Ice Age began at the end of a 226-million-year-long greenhouse period. This last climate change to the colder extreme caused ice to form at Earth's polar caps, which however, took 26 Ma to reach present levels. As this occurred, Earth's climate regularly **oscillated**, moving from cold glacial conditions to relatively warm interglacial periods. The most recent and noticeable oscillations began 130,000 years ago, when the Eemian, an interglacial period, began. This coincided with Adam and Eve's appearance on Earth. They had come into a world of plenty, which enabled them to thrive, and as their numbers grew, so did their communities, which eventually expanded into cities that gained a global reach. With their intellect, they established in prehistory the first civilisation and the first human global empire.

Change came 15,000 years later when Earth's climate oscillated back to its colder state. This became known as the last glacial period that eventually peaked 95,000 years later with the last glacial maximum. Global temperatures then plunged, and Earth froze for 12,000 years. This freeze caused the sea levels to drop by 120 metres and polar ice sheets with glaciers to extend to middle latitudes. At its near end, before the start of the present interglacial period, the Younger Dryas occurred, which led to a world reset. When this cleared and Earth's environment, along with its climate stabilised in its present state, arose the greater human consciousness that exist today.

The Ancients' Internet

The ancients are superior in every respect when compared to humans. They have highly evolved minds, superior intellect, and extraordinary psionic abilities. This, they either had gained or were gifted by having lived hundreds of millions of years. Their abilities enabled them to remote view, visualise, and see what occurs elsewhere without needing to physically be there. They also can read the minds, thoughts, and intentions of and control any lesser being. They have foresight, enabling them to see the likely future and know what is destined to occur. When they communicate, they do this by some means of advanced molecular quantum transfer. They transmit thought messages that can traverse this universe without any loss or distortion. Within their synthesised form, they have enhanced genetics that has stored their vast reservoir of sacred knowledge, which at will they can access with their minds, as it is linked to every cell of their being.

No matter where they are or go, their minds and thoughts remain connected to the one community mind. This is their internet of sorts, which also magnifies their psionic abilities. With the power they can wield, they can do the impossible, answer inconceivable questions, create new realities, open portals to adjoining multiverses, and transfer matter or beings to any place, time, or reality.

Within their out-of-phase realm, they live in their own created reality. There, they have many self-organising and integrated systems, which they had created and placed there. Theses they manifest these into existence, tailored for their specific needs. Each is well beyond our **comprehension** and otherwise impossible to recreate in this reality. We simply cannot imagine or contemplate the intelligence or power they have or what they can do or achieve. They have already answered every conceivable question and accessed all places, times, and locations. They have the means with power to control all there is in this universe, but this, they don't do as this would change the balance of things and tip this world and theirs into chaos.

The End of Reptilian Dominance

The ancients who lived on Earth were unlike humans. Without hands, they relied solely on their gifted superior intellect and psionic abilities. With these gifts, they could manipulate matter. Together, they would merge their minds, **magnify** their abilities so to gain the means to manipulate time and space and do otherwise impossible things. From this came their community mind, a formless entity of pure intelligence that had manifested into existence as an omnipresent being. This entity then found itself when it entered the sixth dimension. Being part of the greater intelligence, it merged and re-joined its greater whole.

The ancients gained by this merge. This had linked their minds directly to unlimited power sources that exist in the sixth dimension. With this, they gained the means to warp and mould reality at both the micro and macro scales. At the micro scale, the ancients could then experiment with creation, with lives' essence, their DNA and genetics. This enabled the ancients to modify their genetics at the sub-atomic scale. By aligning the resonance frequencies of their genetics with the sixth dimension, they found they could separate their essence from their mortal form. With this, they began transforming themselves, migrating into and occupying synthesised bodies.

At the macro scale, the ancients found they could cut through time and space. This enabled them to access the deep past and distant future. In the past, they experienced creation and saw how mass extinctions had progressed life on Earth. In the future, they saw the eventual demise of their reptilian lineage.

Seeing and knowing their end was nigh, the ancients began searching for suitable alternate DNA. They soon realised they needed to create a compatible, suitable lifeform that could replace their synthesised reptilian form. They needed a long-lived lifeform that could attain and retain comparable psionic abilities. This then began their experimentation and genetic manipulation of what was to become mammalian, stem mammals.

Transcending Evolution

The 182 Ma long Age of Reptiles ended with the last mass extinction. With this, **entropy**, the second law of thermodynamics, set in and took hold and began devolving the reptilian-dinosaur lineage, regressing all that once dominated back to a subdued and primitive form.

The ancients, however, were mostly unaffected by this. They had already exited from the cycle of life by migrating to the sixth dimension, their out-of-phase realm. There, they gained the means to transfer their essence and intelligence at will. With this, they gained immortality by discarding their mortal forms and by upgrading themselves into synthesised bodies.

The ancients' transformation, however, was temporary. Their synthesised form needed to be regularly upkept with suitable and compatible genetics. Their form was a mere temporary vessel that time would progressively corrupt and devolve to nothingness, and by knowing stocks of compatible reptilian DNA and genetics would soon diminish and end, they sought to find a more permanent, resilient, and enduring form. This began their quest which would take 229 Ma to fulfil.

The ancients began by experimenting on many species, forcing genetic change, manipulating and mixing all available DNA. This process needed 51 Ma for the first mammalian lifeform to emerge. This was a godsend for the mammalian species as this began their ascension into dominance. From this, a new era also emerged, along with the Age of Mammals. It then took another 123 Ma of forced evolution to produce the first primate and a further 48.7 Ma for the first hominin. This then culminated 6 Ma later with the AMH, which then begun the next phase of their transformation, the replacement of the synthesised reptilian genetics with mammalian.

Evolved Communal Intelligence

The ancients' lineage emerged from a small reptilian-dinosaur species that survived the Permian-Triassic mass extinction. They were one of few survivors who quickly learned their survival depended on collaboration and combining resources. Together, they overcame their individual vulnerabilities. This transformed them, enhanced their abilities, and made them into a formidable species that could then overpower any adversary.

The ancients could only exist together. They were a close-knit community that hunted instinctively, in packs, swarmed like birds, using their speed, cunning, and intelligence to outmanoeuvre their prey and predators. Their constant interactions and instinctive collaboration soon gifted them telepathic abilities. This expanded their awareness and enabled them to communicate by thought.

By turning their minds to the environment, the ancients gained the ability to remote view. By tampering with the physical constraints of this world, they also gained the ability to levitate and alter matter. This somehow also changed the structure of their minds, gifting them enhanced psionic abilities. As a collective, they could then magnify their abilities by combining and merging their minds, from which emerged their community mind. This then enabled them to do the **extraordinary**.

The ancients' reality then changed when they opened portals to other worlds within this universe. This transported them to the sixth dimension where they met similar beings, who became their brethren. This was where they also learned to elevate themselves, to the seventh dimension, so to gain access to the parallel universes.

The Merge of Minds

Life on Earth needed 15 Ma to again flourish after the Great Dying. From the ashes emerged a mutated reptilian-dinosaur lineage that soon evolved to become superior, dominant, and intelligent. These were the ancients.

The ancients were the first on Earth to gain and master psionic abilities. With this, they could manipulate matter and control the prehistoric megafauna that then existed. Time had progressively enhanced their abilities; eventually gifting them the means to open portals into the fourth, fifth and sixth dimensions. It had taken them 9.4 Ma to achieve this. There, they found an out-of-phase realm, a place that housed communities of equally intelligent beings with comparable psionic abilities.

Psionic powers are rare and highly valued in this universe. These are needed to enter the out-of-phase realm. On entry, beings must traverse past the powerful one community mind that exists in the realm. This ethereal entity is the protector of the realm. Entry is solely dependent on the psionic powers of individuals, who must first link and merge with this one community mind to prove their worth. This, the ancients manipulated by merging their community mind with this greater entity. Integrating this merge greatly benefited all. This established a feedback loop that began to resonate with frequencies that enhanced abilities, enabling individuals with psionic abilities to do impossible things. With this, the ancients found they could travel anywhere, to every conceivable place, including adjoining multiverses. They could also materialise new materials into existence, including operational systems that then enhanced the realm.

Genetic Adaptation

After 9 Ma on Earth, the ancients' mortal form had reached the end of its evolutionary path. They could no longer reproduce naturally or artificially. Their genetics had mutated and began to progressively devolve. They had become nonbinary, asexual, and genderless beings who were then destined to fade into history. Providence, however, intervened and prevented their demise.

The ancients found ways to manipulate their genetics with their combined psionic abilities and their community mind. They could peer deep into, access, and manipulate their DNA at the sub-atomic level. This enabled them to progressively upgrade themselves, enhancing their genetics and bodies from within. Their experimentations then expanded to include other species, which they manipulated to produce **hybrid** beings so to replicate their form. This provided the ancients with harvestable stock of primitive yet fertile, robust, resilient, enhanced, and compatible genetics, which they used and implanted into themselves so to futureproof their race.

Eventually, the ancients also gained the means to disconnect and separate their minds, soul, and essence from their flesh. With the hybrid avatars, synthesised bodies they occupied, they attained virtual immortality, needing only to upkeep or replace these with new, enhanced, upgraded versions.

The ancients had made us an integral part of this – we became one of their manipulations. They had forced evolution to rapidly progress our lineage, and as our lineage evolved, they progressively reengineered our genetics, at times switching on or off certain genes so to produce new, improved hybrid variants so to culminate with an ultimate, most enduring form which they could use. We became the outcome of this.

Out-of-Phase Existence

The ancients do not need to reside on Earth to thrive. Their out-of-phase realm provides them with everything they need and all they want. This place has also enhanced their abilities and gifted them the means to manipulate all there is and do otherwise impossible things.

Physical laws within the sixth dimension are vastly different. There exists an altered state that has varying space and time correlations with the lower dimensions. What is seen appears to be in a state of flux, is transparent, fluid, in constant motion, vibrating to some alternating frequency. With a transfixed gaze, what is seen progressively extends to the sub-atomic structure. There, every molecule and atom can be reached. As these come to focus, each part can then be touched, moved, separated, rearranged, or manipulated.

The concept of distance is not relevant in this realm. Space can be seen continually folding into itself as portals magically appear when willed into existence. These portals make everything and every place accessible – all places, planets, stars, universes, and multiverses. Anywhere can be reached from here.

Within this realm, the ancients have connected themselves to a ubiquitous yet inexhaustible quantum power supply. They have purposefully reengineered their internal genetic structure so to attune to this and to the resonance emitted by the one community mind. The power from this alignment, when wielded, can redefine matter and create new realities. With this, they have assembled – atom by atom, molecule by molecule – otherwise impossible structures with many living machines, and to fuel their time travel machines, they reassembled and reconfigured element 115, one of the rarest, most unstable, and yet powerful elements. They stabilised this by changing its half-life from 0.65 seconds to infinity. With this, they gained the ability to travel beyond time and space.

The Ancients' Power

True power lies within the mind, with intellect and psionic abilities. This is the ancients' power source. Their evolved mind, superior intellect, and enhanced psionic abilities enable them to do all things, venture to all places, enter forbidden territories, and travel to adjoining multiverses.

The power wielded by the ancients has made them into true gods. A mere thought of theirs can

overpower

any lesser being and primitive mind. When they combine and merge their minds, they gain the additional ability to create and move this world.

For hundreds of millions of years, the ancients had manipulated the genetics of species on Earth and throughout in this universe. As they had done this, they also extensively spread their seed, implanted their DNA to emerging life so to ensure future compatibility. What they manipulated, they then forced to rapidly evolve, physically and biologically.

The ancients had sought to attain a form with functioning limbs, useful hands, and an upright body whose metabolism, appearance, and body form was suitable to them. They ventured deep within mammalian genetics, progressively manipulating the sub-atomic structure, the essence of life, to achieve this. From this emerged the form they had sought, the AMHs, their first manipulated species with sufficient intellect. They then had to enhance the mind of the AMH until it could support and retain their psionic abilities.

The Ancients' Legacy

The ancients reside in a realm the exists outside time and space. This realm's altered reality enables the ancients to reach everywhere in this universe. They see all that exists and know all that occur, and with their psionic abilities, they can manipulate all there is. This has made the ancients into omnipresent and omnipotent beings. They are the **true gods**.

Everything that exists in the third dimension – space, time, and life – is all within their reach, and all these, they can manipulate and alter from the sixth dimension. This is what the ancients have done and are still doing. They have tampered with all. They have slowed and hastened time to travel both to the past and future. They have manipulated the fabric of life, the genetics of species so to progress life for their benefit. They have quickened evolutionary processes by forcing change and the adaption of species so life gains sufficient resilience to survive their manipulation with implants. This, they have done to native fauna in hundreds of habitable worlds so to make all life compatible in this universe. Now they simply wait for their manipulation to evolve, mature, and gain intellect.

One day, in the distant future, possibly many hundreds of millions of years from now, all the manipulated life in this universe is bound to unite and connect as one. We are part of this. We have the same DNA the ancients spread to other habitable worlds. This has made us part of all that exists in this universe. This is the ancients' legacy.

THE HUMAN STORY

Then the Lord God formed man from dust and breathed into his nostrils the breath of life. Man then became a living creature. (Genesis 2:7)

When the earliest primates emerged, Earth was still in its last greenhouse phase. This was, 21 Ma before the climate would change to its present Late Cenozoic Ice Age state. When this occurred, the ensuing coldness led to rapid evolutionary change. What adapted best to the cold and fluctuating temperatures thrived, from which, 28 Ma later, came the first hominins, needing only a further 6 Ma to become AMHs.

The ancients' manipulations had partly enabled this. They had forced evolution on the hominins to accelerate, quicken, and produce a most enduring form. The earliest AMHs still, however, needed a further 185,000 years to mature, to gain their final form. This came with Adam, who received the ancients' last upgrade. He became the ancients' prodigy, having both the genetic form with intellect that the ancients had sought.

Adam's legacy began when he exited Eden. He left, tasked with populating Earth so to establish a harvestable DNA source for the ancients.

Adam's arrival on Earth coincided with the start of the **Eemian**, a 15,000 year-long interglacial period. The relative warmth of the time was much like today, which enabled Adam and kin to establish themselves and prepare for what was to come. Change came when the last glacial period began, leading to a 105,000-year-long freeze. When this peaked, the ensuing coldness from the last glacial maximum wrought havoc, decimated food sources, and lowered sea levels by more than 120 metres. This, however, did not greatly impact Adam's legacy. His descendants had already proven themselves to be both resilient and enduring; however, they were not prepared for what came next: the Younger Dryas.

The Great Hominin Experiment

When the ancients began searching for a new, enduring lifeform, they proceeded to experiment on many species, including stem mammals. This lifeform proved the most amenable and enduring, being able to morph into mammals and then primates, hominins, and finally AMHs. Natural selection and evolutionary processes then tested each new variant form, forcing each to compete to survive and persist. Each then sought to outlast their rivals so to become the successor.

The ancients helped our ancestors become the key active participant of this process. Their genetic manipulations and upgrades enhanced our lineage, which eventually progressed the AMH to Adam, who was what the ancients had sought. He had a similar lifespan to the ancients, with comparable intellect and psionic abilities. This then marked the end of the ancients' upgrade of our lineage as they feared any further enhancements would produce a **superhuman** race whose abilities would surpass theirs. To avoid this, the ancients placed limits on Adam's genetics so he could neither pass his longevity nor his psionic abilities to his descendants. This reduced the human lifespan tenfold, from 1,000 to 100 years, and limited mind access to 10 per cent so no psionic abilities could be attained. What Adam did, however, was gift his descendants an enhanced form with superior intellect that was sufficient to establish his legacy and the first cultured civilisation on Earth.

Superior intellect differentiated Adam's descendants from all other variant hominins and the lesser evolved AMHs. Adam's seed and genetics would soon enlighten these hunters and gatherers so to enable them to integrate into his society. This eventually homogenised the human population, producing what exists today.

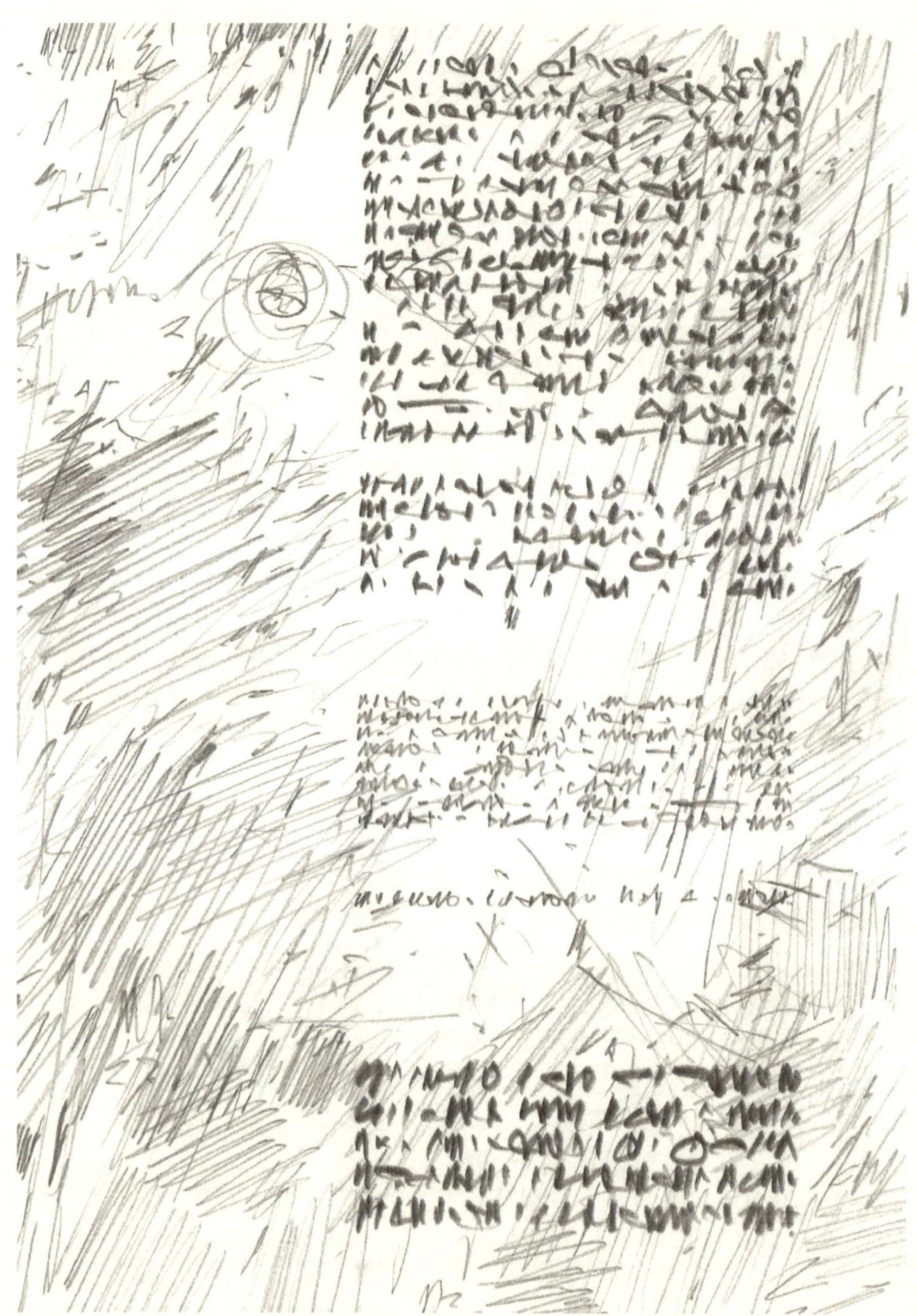

Human Evolution

A complex yet fast-tracked speciation–hybridisation process forced the primates and then hominins to evolve continually and rapidly so to produce a most enduring form. There were multiple inflection points which each variant form had to endure and traverse. Those with dominant genes outcompeted and then absorbed other variant forms. This was natural selection at work, seeking to find the fittest, who could then dominate.

Cycles of hybridisation were followed by reproductive isolation periods and interbreeding. As this progressed certain hominins, the genetic recombination and mutation processes with chromosomal abnormalities also doomed many. Only the most resilient genes, features, and dominant anatomical characteristics were retained and passed to subsequent generations. This was a process that continually absorbed or discarded the less successful genes and variant forms.

From this emerged the first AMHs 315,000 years ago. They appeared at a time when many other variant forms still existed. The first AMHs, however, were still primitive and needed time to attain their final form and intellect. Then came Adam, who emerged 185,000 years later as the most evolved AMH. It however took another 100,000 years for the AMHs to become the sole and **fittest** survivors. This occurred 30,000 years ago, when the last of the lineage of the Neanderthals disappeared.

Despite all the genetic mutations, upgrades, and biological changes that occurred from the first primate to the final AMH form, the human DNA remains 99 per cent identical to that of the primate–chimpanzee lineage. The true difference lies in the gifted non-coded DNA that the ancients manipulated within us.

This Hominin Lineage

What forced the hominins to undergo rapid evolutionary change? Why were there so many variants? Was natural selection at work – or some manipulation?

Some of the many variant species that emerged included the following:

- *Sahelanthropus tchadensis*, 6.3 Ma ago
- *Orrorin tugenensis*, 6 Ma ago
- *Ardipithecus kadabba*, 5.8 Ma ago
- *Ardipithecus ramidus*, 4.4 Ma ago
- *Australopithecus anamensis*, 4.2 Ma ago
- *Australopithecus afarensis*, 3.85 Ma ago
- *Kenyanthropus platyops*, 3.5 Ma ago
- *Australopithecus africanus*, 3.3 Ma ago
- *Paranthropus aethiopicus*, 2.3 Ma ago
- *Paranthropus boisei*, 2.3 Ma ago
- *Homo habilis*, 2.33 Ma ago
- *Homo rudolfensis*, 1.9 Ma ago
- *Homo ergaster*, 1.8 Ma ago
- *Homo erectus*, 1.89 Ma ago
- *Denisova hominin*, 765,000 years ago
- *Homo heidelbergensis*, 700,000 years ago
- *Homo rhodesiensis*, 400,000 years ago
- *Homo **neanderthalensis**,* 400,000 years ago
- *Homo sapiens*, 315,000 years ago

The Earliest Modern Human

Natural selection and a hybridisation process had progressed hominins to AMHs. The AMHs were one of many variant versions of hominins the ancients' upgrades had produced and then forced to compete against each other. The ancients did this so a most enduring form would emerge. It was only when the AMHs had sufficiently matured and began outcompeting their rival and dominating the landscape that the ancients noticed them. The ancients then chose this lineage to receive their final upgrade in the Garden of Eden. This then also guaranteed their survival.

And after you have suffered a little while, the God of all grace, who has called you to his eternal glory in Christ, will himself restore, confirm, strengthen, and establish you. (Peter 5:10)

The AMHs taken to the ancients' lair were experimented on, manipulated, and upgraded. Some were gifted with high intellect, some with longevity, and others with psionic abilities. The ancients did this to ensure the genetics of the AMH was suitable for their use. Eventually, from this emerged Adam, their most enhanced form, a person who had attained longevity, high intellect, and psionic abilities. Adam also had the genetics and form the ancients had sought. This made him special, the first, who would then be placed on Earth to establish a **harvestable** source of suitable human DNA.

Other, older variant hominins such as the Denisovans and Neanderthals had long failed to progress. Inbreeding had corrupted their genetics and doomed their race. When the Younger Dryas decimated this world, all these older variant forms had already disappeared. The few surviving descendants of Adam were then forced to collaborate with the remaining, lesser evolved AMHs. Eventually, they passed their genetics to them, gifting their offspring their superior intellect. This then enabled humans to journey far, expand their tribes, and grow their numbers. This then also secured the ancients' DNA source.

Humans of Prehistory

We have a longer prehistory than recorded history. The AMH emerged 315,000 years ago as the last variant hominin version. Adam, who then came 185,000 years later, was the last AMH to receive an upgrade from the ancients. The ancients had transformed him into the ultimate AMH, an upgraded human, who was superior, the most evolved, and comparable to the ancients.

Adam's legacy was his superior intellect, which he passed to all of his descendants. His descendants were the extraordinary humans from prehistory. They established the first global empire that connected all continents. They had no need for reading or writing as their high intellect had gifted them telepathic abilities. The ancients also gave some psionic abilities, albeit limited, so they would not they need to develop technologies or utilise sciences. With psionic abilities, they manipulated matter with their minds, created structures that turned into glorious cities and vessels that enabled global travel.

The ancients had tasked **Adam** with populating Earth with his seed. This, his legacy, continued for 117,000 years, ending with the Younger Dryas. This was a global event that decimated the entire empire his descendants had established. It ended civilisation and changed everything. The few that survived were forced to restart.

The Younger Dryas event erased everything that existed in prehistory. Everything was first destroyed by floods that came from ice melt water and then, was submerged with the 120-metre sea level rise that followed. Tales of this flood exist in scripture, while the only remaining conclusive proof exists with the Piri Reis map. This map, drawn in 1513, used information that is at least 115,000 years old. This map dates back to the Eemian, before the start of last glacial period, a time when the northern coast of Antarctica was ice free.

Adam

Adam's genetics were suitable to begin the ancients' transformation from a reptilian to a mammalian synthesised form. Adam was the outcome of the ancients' manipulation. He was what they had long sought.

Adam was special. According to Hebrew Scriptures, Adam lived for **930 years** and had fifty-six children.

Adam was the most evolved and advanced human who ever lived. He was both the alpha and the omega, the first and last of his kind. He had comparable intellect with psionic abilities as the ancients, which made him their final creation. The ancients then ensured neither his longevity nor his psionic abilities would be passed to others unless arranged by them.

Adam's legacy ended in 10,800 BC with the Younger Dryas. This was the event that decimated all that existed in prehistory. The few that managed to survive were then forced to collaborate, pool their abilities and resources so to endure the ensuing turmoil and later be able to recommence civilisation. As this occurred, Adam's direct descendants became the agents of the ancients. They were the *chosen one*s, given the authority to rule on Earth, which they did with impunity.

The ancients' requirements were simple. They needed to re-establish a civilised society so to enable population growth while also ensuring humans remained forever divided so they could never amass as one global power. This was achieved by establishing and then reinforcing borders and differing cultures and by instilling varying beliefs with scriptures and gods, all of which persists to this day.

The Exit from Eden

Why did Adam and Eve leave the Garden of Eden?

Was Eden a paradise or a prison?

Were they banished or allowed to go on their own accord?

For an eternity, the ancients took species to their lair, their out-of-phase realm. There, they manipulated genetics, altering these to make species compatible and progress these to more enduring forms. From this came primates and then hominins and finally the AMHs. The most notable AMH was Adam, who came directly to Earth from the Garden of Eden, the ancients'

laboratory.

At the end of each manipulation, each upgraded variant form was released so natural selection would play its part. There were many hominin versions, each manipulated, further enhanced, and each was forced to compete with all that existed. This was how the hominins also gained resilience and matured rapidly. With this, it only took 6.3 Ma for AMHs to emerge, a shortened period compared to the previous step which had taken 49 Ma for hominins to evolve from primates.

The AMHs were the most evolved. They were the upgraded version to all that previously existed and thereby could easily outcompete the older variant hominins. They, however, still needed one final upgrade to become what the ancients wanted. This came with Adam, who was gifted with the genetics, intellect, and abilities that the ancients had long sought. Adam then became the outcome of the ancients' manipulations, their prodigy, the last AMH to receive an upgrade and whose lineage God then chose to populate this world.

The Key to the Kingdom

What is the meaning and symbolism behind the shape of the key?

The key represents power and control. Captives held in the ancients' lair saw this shape and felt how this wielded power that controlled and manipulated them.

The key represents who the ancients were and are. The shape, with blade facing downwards, represents an upright ancient. The head of the key is the face looking forward with open eyes and a gaping mouth. The lower blade represents the ancients' genitalia, their seed, which was used to upgrade Adam. This made us who we are.

I will give you the keys of the **kingdom of heaven**. (Matthew 16:19)

Memories of the symbolism behind the key lie deep within our subconscious. We have unknowingly allowed this to manifest into reality, becoming an integral part of our lives. The keys we now all hold and carry are the constant subconscious reminders of what the ancients did to us and are still doing.

The symbolic key can be seen everywhere and throughout recorded human history. The best known is the Egyptian Ankh cross, which was proclaimed to epitomise power by having the authority and control over life and the afterlife. From the many historical deities, mythical creatures, and iconic religious figureheads that are shown carrying symbolic keys, Janus, the two-faced Roman god, is possibly the best known. His keys were used to open life to a new time and beginning. This transition has since become the new year by which the first month of the Gregorian calendar is now named.

The ultimate key, however, is within our mind. This is what the ancients have – psionic abilities, the power to determine fate. Adam had this. With this, he was able to exit Eden without the ancients' help. Most of recent history has this key depicted as our third eye, which exists dormant in our minds. This is the key that will gift us access to sacred knowledge and bring us the salvation and the immortality we desire.

Human Prehistory Achievements and Civilisation

Adam's legacy lasted 117,000 years. It began with the 15,000 year-long Eemien, a time of plenty. This then changed to hard and uncompromising times with the 105,000-year-long last glacial period. In 10,800 BC, the coincidence that occurred with the end of this period, together with end of the last glacial maximum and the Younger Dryas, ended Adam's legacy.

Before this occurred, during the intervening years, in prehistory, Adam's descendants had established civilisation with a global reach. This was a time when sea levels were 120 metres lower than today and ice sheets connected Asia with the Americas.

All the achievements made in prehistory were enabled by their superior intellect which Adam's genetics had gifted his descendants. The ancients had also ensured their success by gifting, at times, psionic abilities to certain individuals so they could progress their society. Many impressive coastal cities were built, all linked to a global empire connected by sea travel. The best known was Atlantis, which showed the world a powerful dynasty with no equal.

Adam's legacy and dynasty, however, were not prepared for the devastation that the **Younger Dryas** unleashed. The reset this event caused destroyed all that existed in prehistory. After the destruction, the sea level rise then consumed Adam's legacy, dynasty, and global empire, removing all traces of what had been achieved and what had existed.

The Younger Dryas

Reality is stranger than fiction.

The Younger Dryas led to a sequence of events that unleashed complete devastation on Earth. This began as Earth traversed through the Taurid Meteor Stream, which repeats at the same time of each zodiac great year, every 25,772 years. This event became **CATACLYSMIC** as hundreds of meteors rained down on Earth at the end of the last glacial maximum.

This occurred 12,823 years ago. This was when Earth began to warm as the climate shifted from its glacial maximum to a warmer interglacial state. The comets that rained down caused the glacial ice sheets to break and release melt water. The flooding that ensued covered the landscape with mud and rocks and destroyed everything in its path. Earth's climate then oscillated between extremes for 1,300 years. Short deep freezes with glacial conditions were followed with periods of elevated greenhouse temperatures.

Eventually, the climate stabilised into the present warmer, interglacial state. Sea levels then rose by 120 metres. As Earth's coastlines receded, water inundated the lowlands, which then covered all traces of human prehistory.

This began a new era for humans. Survivors of this last climate change with sea level rise were then forced to come together, join forces so to persist in a decimated world. The few survivors of Adam's descendants were instrumental in forcing the many competing clans and tribes of the lesser evolved AMH to merge. From this arose new communities, which had integrated disparate, displaced peoples, homogenising the human population. This is how we became, from this final merge of humans. This had reset history and began our time.

God's Fruit and Wrath

God, on the sixth day of creation, created man in his image, and from this came the female. God then blessed the couple, gave them dominion over all living things, and told them to be fruitful and multiply. They could eat all fruits except one. Forbidden to them was the one fruit from the tree of knowledge.

Adam was the outcome of God's manipulations. He was God's final act. This was what the ancients achieved and wanted. Adam's gifts, however, were then restricted to others as the ancients did not want these to be passed to his descendants.

The calamity that the Younger Dryas caused had not truly ended Adam's legacy as this had led to the worldwide spread of his genetics, his seed, which eventually homogenised the human population. The intermixing of Adam's surviving **descendants** with the lesser evolved AMHs led to the awakening of the greater human consciousness. To avoid chaos, the ancients intervened, proclaiming themselves to be gods so they could control and rule the growing human population.

Through religion, the ancients set rules dictating how life was to be lived on Earth. With the sacred knowledge they imparted began agriculture and horticulture, and humans learned to domesticate animals. From this emerged communities, towns, cities, and a civilised humanity. This set the framework that then guided how life was to be lived, tying humanity forevermore to the land and servitude. This was purposefully done to encourage growth and establish a plentiful, regenerative supply of harvestable human DNA for the ancients.

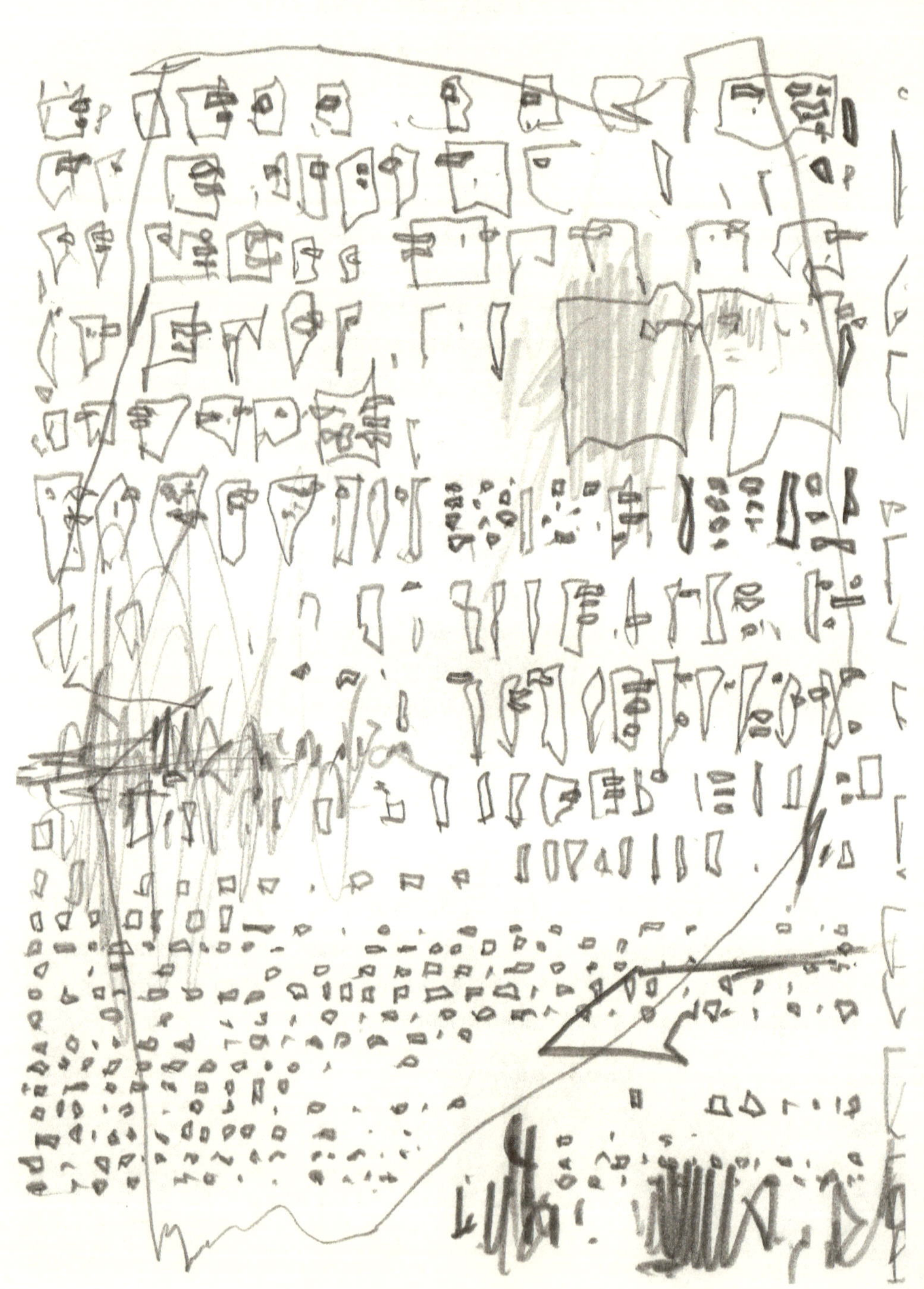

God's Nature

The truth is we were not created in God's image. Rather, the ancients created us while they sought to transform themselves to mammalian. We are the outcome of a process of genetic and DNA manipulation that predated the first mammalian form. The ancients facilitated this by fast-tracking change, accelerating evolutionary processes so an enduring, compatible form would emerge. Their manipulations bypassed millions of years of otherwise necessary evolutionary time. From this emerged many new hybrid forms, all in rapid succession, each with enhanced genetics. This process, however, did not change their nature or enhance their minds. Nor did this process remove or quell primitive traits.

This has become our dilemma. We have an evolved form with a largely undeveloped mind. We have retained many primal urges with sinful desires. These have given us a self-serving, unrepentant nature together with a vengeful, **unforgiving soul.**

History has recorded what we have done, harming both ourselves and this Earth. We are merely copying what the ancients have done to us.

We manipulate every aspect of Earth and experiment on lesser evolved species, pushing many to their limits, either for our pleasure or for our benefit. This has forced many species to adapt unnecessarily and change so to persist in this human-dominated world. Like the ancients, we have quickened evolutionary change, but unlike them, we are unable to determine or set our destiny. Without realising, what we have done, has inadvertently shortened our time. We have forced a new future to rapidly emerge, one that we may not like. Soon, this, what we have started, will accelerate and will likely take life beyond us.

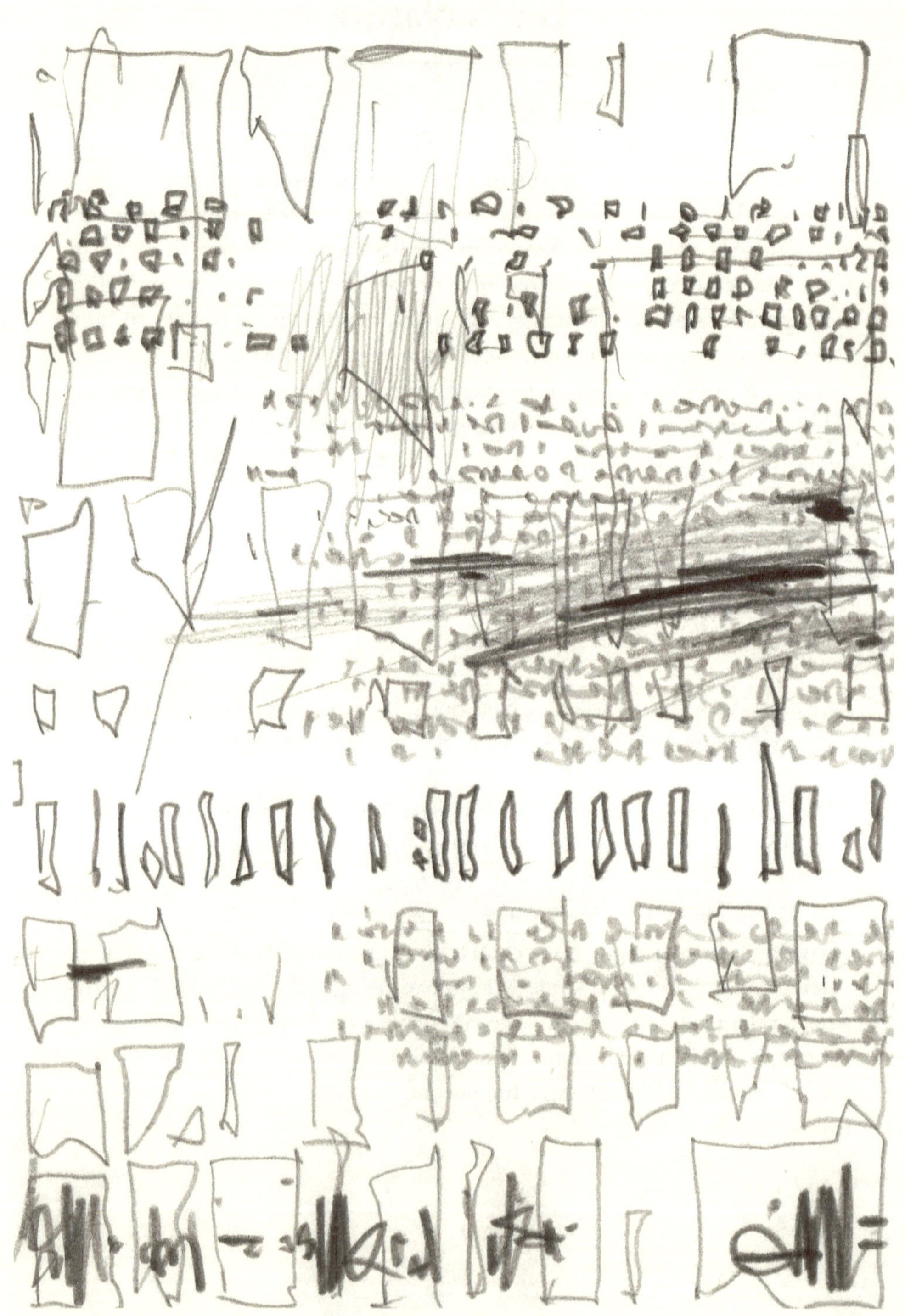

Human Potential

We became the sole hominins survivor when the last of the Neanderthal lineage disappeared 40,000 years ago. We then became the outcome of the ancients' 6.3-million-year-long manipulation of the hominin lineage. All other hominins either perished or were absorbed by the process. The ancients had planned and enabled this. They did this to produce an enduring form that had the intellect and stamina to outcompete and overcome stronger and older rivals.

The ancients had **engineered** the human form for this. They ensure it had great potential, although most of it is now dormant within, waiting for some evolutionary trigger or further manipulation to awaken. We all have what the ancients gave Adam with their last upgrade in the Garden of Eden 130,000 years ago. We have the same DNA that has been made for a 1000-year lifespan but reprogrammed for a hundred. We have a mind that can attain, retain, and apply psionic abilities, but this has been blocked by the ancients. They governed this by restricting access to 10 per cent of our minds. We must therefore wait until we either mature or gain the technology to access and release the dormant parts that lie within us.

We can all aspire to what Adam had and was gifted. He was the first and last of his kind. He was the ultimate human, a superhuman, who had lived to 930 years. Having full access to his mind, he could access his extensive psionic abilities, which were comparable to those of the ancients. His intellect, which he passed to his descendants, enabled civilisation to be established in prehistory, flourish, span the globe, and last for 117,000 years.

Our Inbuilt Bias

We have an unquenchable, sinful desire and thirst that drives us with greed to possess or decimate all we can.

It had taken 178 Ma of manipulations for the ancients to produce a suitable mammalian lifeform. Adam was the outcome of this. He had attained the ultimate human form. Adam, however, had come before his time. The accelerated evolutionary process had gifted him evolved genetics and high intellect, but this had kept his primitive and immature nature unchanged. With this dilemma and fearing what might eventuate, the ancients then reprogrammed Adam's seed and genetics, governing his abilities so not to pass these to his descendants.

This is also the dilemma we all have. We cannot control all we think and do. We are easily swayed and influenced by desires, driven by primitive urges, along with destructive and selfish wants. These, we cannot easily quell. When we self-assess, we invariable find we care for none more than for ourselves, and when we reflect, we find we have done many stupid things without considering consequences.

Alone, without **guidance** or leadership, we flounder. We were designed to rely on others, to be led and told what to do. But when we look at our society, we find there is no one in complete control. Those who do lead us often tap into their primitive nature so to overwhelm and then decimate everything that stands in their way. This same nature our ancestors used to hunt to extinction all they feared, including the woolly mammoth, the giant deer, the sabre-toothed cat, the cave lion, the European leopard, and all the other variant hominins. Without these, we now only fight ourselves, resulting with unending wars that at times, take us to the brink of imminent annihilation. This is also a nature that often subconsciously and secretly wishes to end this, our damned human existence. This is who we are, both as individuals and as a society. This is the state of our immaturity, our nature and mind, which is likely to remain so until we transcend this mortal state.

Our Destructive Nature

Whilst Steven Dawkins gazed at the stars to understand the universe, we looked deep within our souls and hearts and saw who we really were.

Humanity has been indoctrinated and programmed to forever be subjugated and controlled. This was done so we readily accept and follow those who rule and lead us and do what is expected and what we are told.

This indoctrination began when religion merged with how we were to live. This redefined what we did and who we were. Our ancestors were told how to harvest from the land and how to accumulate property and wealth. This was so structured so it became an inescapable lifestyle that enslaved people with greed and thoughts of entitlement. This then set the framework for how life was to be lived forevermore.

Be fruitful and multiply *and replenish the earth and subdue it: and have dominion over the fish of the sea and over the fowl of the air and over every living thing that moveth upon the earth.* (Genesis 1:28)

This is exactly what we did. Without questioning or without finding balances on Earth – not with ourselves, with other species, or with the environment – we did exactly what religion told us to do. Even now, we simply continue to consume and populate this world. Everything else is relegated to inconsequential and immaterial things that are to be taken, possessed, consumed, and then disposed. With this, everything is progressively transformed from its natural state to commodities, consumable products, waste, and more people. If this is God's will, it then is also God's will that we cause misery, suffering, and harm to this world.

The real irony is that we simply fail to realise what we do is exactly what has been done to us. What we have done to others, the ancients had done to us. They had made us and then domesticated us so we became their resource for their consumption.

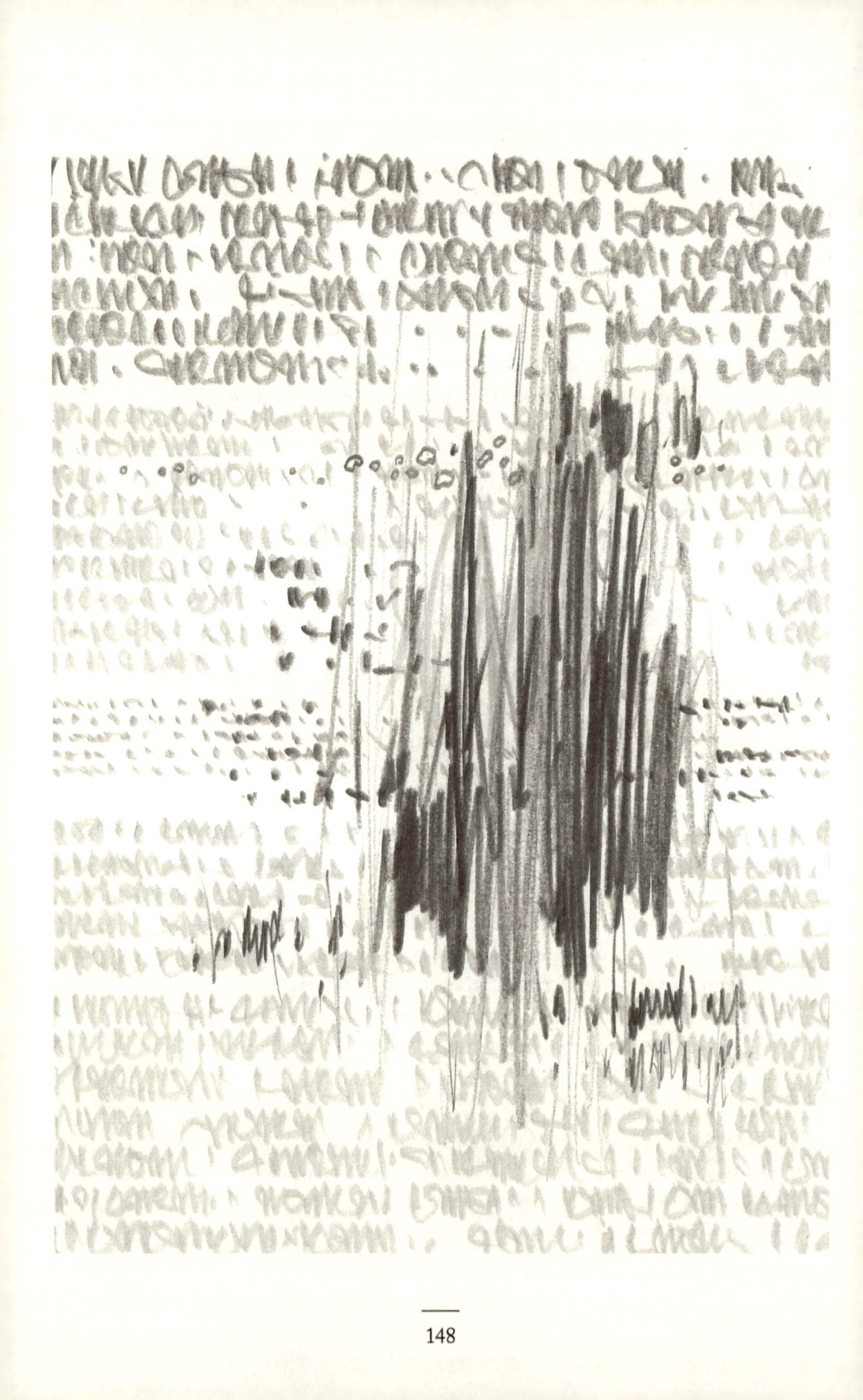

Embedded Memories of God

The ancients have always controlled humans. They controlled the earliest humans with their psionic powers. A mere thought made them succumb to their every wish. However, this proved difficult as deep concentration was required to maintain a mind link with these unruly primitives. Nor could these early humans be controlled en masse as they would only congregate in small groups and had already dispersed worldwide.

Then came Adam, the most evolved human, gifted with high intellect. For 117,000 years, Adam's kin and descendants lived separately from other lesser evolved AMHs. This was so arranged by the ancients to enable Adam's genetics to mature and prepare for what was to come. Change then came with the Younger Dryas, which forced a decimated human population to regroup and homogenise. The ancients had prepared Adam's surviving descendants for this. They were trained as priests and given the authority to rule, enforce laws, and establish God's kingdom on Earth.

With this mandate, priests created sanctuaries that attracted survivors and displaced people. There, these appointed priests imparted their sacred knowledge to a captive population. The ancients helped by systematically manipulating the minds of the general population, embedding false and doctored beliefs, and, at times, changing the recollections of events so to suit their agenda. With this, the construct of God and God worshipping were established. This then became part of the framework for how life was to be lived on Earth – by abiding by God's law.

Many remnants of this same religion persist to this day. We believe God is our saviour and will deliver us from evil. This otherwise unbelievable notion has become an ingrained global belief. Only abductees who have seen the ancients' lair know the truth. There in heaven, an abyss exists, complete with chambers full of overwhelming fire and brimstone that has been specially reserved for humans. Being there and seeing this, the realisation comes that there is no saviour God, and nor will forgiveness or redemption be found in His kingdom.

Our Prayers

Do our prayers reach You, God?

Our primitive voices and minds can only broadcast inefficient and ineffective messages. There is no real substance in our thoughts – nor with what we think. These immediately disperse and fade and are lost to the surrounding ether. This highlights the futility and redundancy of prayer.

Prayers are promoted by priests and religion to reinforce the notion that God is available and that we all can have a personal connection with Him. The reality is prayers are unnecessary as God already knows everything. God already knows all we will say, all that is in our hearts, all we have done, and all that we will do.

Thy will be done.

God's Presence

If we humans are so special, why did God take 4.5 Ga to create us?

After the big bang, it had taken 13.7 Ga for the first AMH, *Homo sapiens*, to appear. The AMH was the last step in a long evolutionary journey. Since then, for 315,000 years AMHs have existed. This is the briefest moment, the smallest fraction of time, in all of Earth's history.

On the sixth day, God created man and woman.

The biblical story of creation has no straight-line evolution that leads to humans. Undoubtedly, many variant ancestral forms emerged before us. We are the last and thereby, the most evolved, and the most intelligent. We, however, are mere newcomers, part of the unending cyclical journey that regularly renews and recycles life.

All life is on this same journey. Evolution forces continual change so to progress life. At times, it gifts intelligence with special abilities, which can be used to shortcut and exit this cycle of life. The ancients did this when they migrated to the sixth dimension. There, they gained immortality and became

eternal and omnipresent

beings that gained the ability to see all there is.

With their gifted abilities, the ancients also gained the means to create and manipulate life. In their lair, a nursery of sorts, in the Garden of Eden, humans then emerged. This was where they conducted their experiments and manipulated our flesh. This was where we became human and where they then tasked Adam with populating Earth. They are our creators, our gods, who now monitor us so we progress and abide by their laws.

All that happened is still happening. What they do is well beyond our comprehension as it is something we don't realise is happening to us. Our governed minds are programmed not to see or acknowledge all that occurs. The reality that exists is well beyond what we think is real. This is something we have been conditioned to dismiss so not to question God's work. Only God knows best.

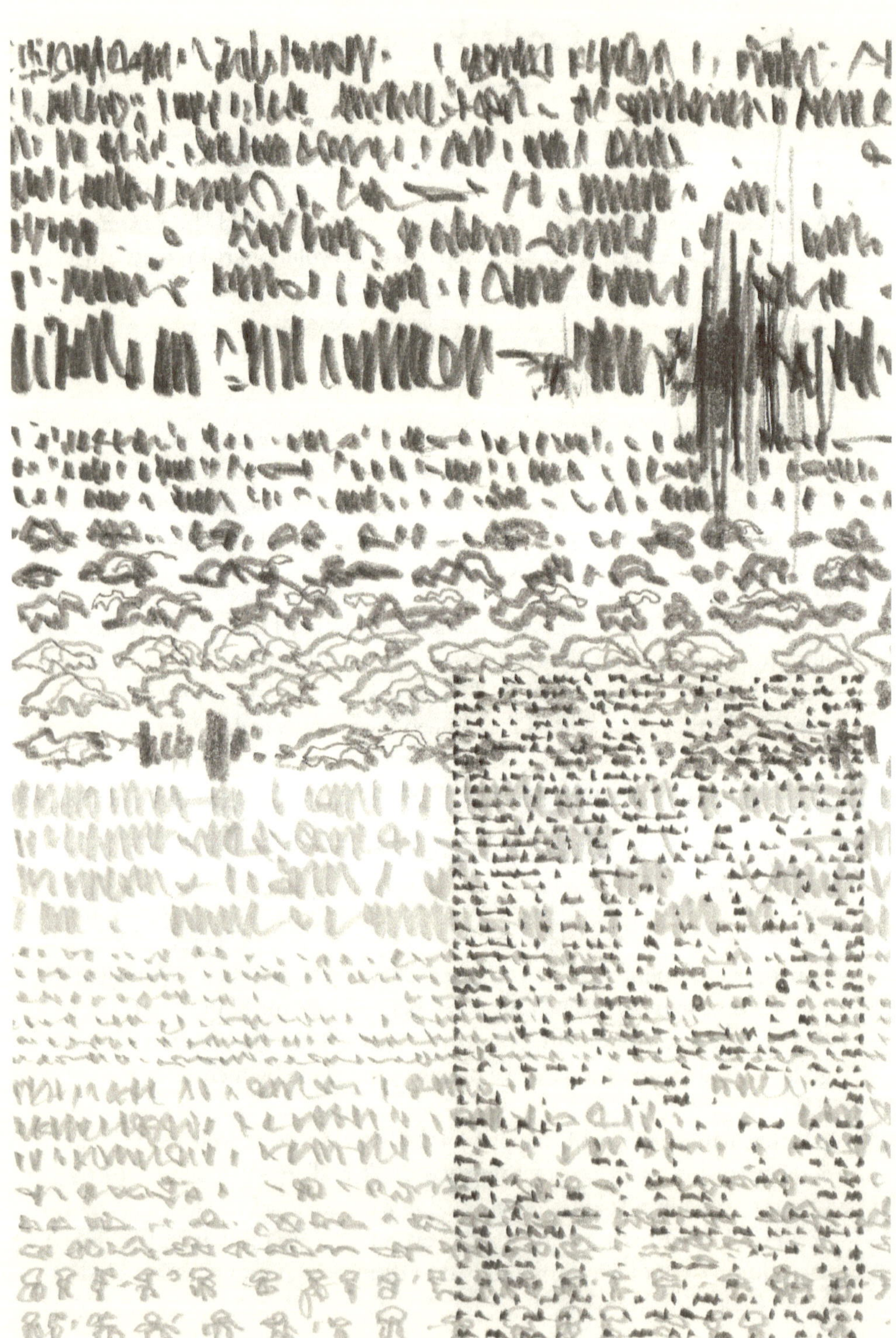

The Longing and Return of God

It is written that Adam was created in God's image and had an honoured status in God's family. He had lived in God's presence, in His dominion, and it was God that expelled him when he ate from the tree of knowledge. The reality, however, was different. Adam did not sin or succumb to evil, and neither was he banished from God's kingdom.

Eden was the ancients' **laboratory** where Adam was pieced together with the genetics of many variant hominins that the ancients had combined. The ancients found with Adam what they needed. Adam was a superhuman, having comparable psionic abilities as the ancients and a lifespan that exceeded a thousand years. It had taken the ancients 221 Ma to achieve this, a mammalian bipedal form that they could use to create their synthesised bodies.

Adam, however, still had a primitive mind and nature. The ancients feared this as they did not want an unruly race of superhumans to emerge from Adam's seed. To avoid this, they placed limits on Adam's seed so he could not pass his gifts to his descendants.

The true nature of humans became apparent when Cain killed his brother, Abel. This then became a common human trait as it started unending series of conflicts and wars that have continued to this day. This is a trait that cannot easily be quelled or changed with genetic manipulation. All that can be done is to coerce the human mind to submit to rule. Religion was then used to reinforce this and ensure we abide by God's rule.

Religion demands we completely surrender to God. This was reinforced when Yahweh met Moses, when His only begotten son, Jesus, met his believers, and when Mohammed introduced the Qur'an to his followers. With these, an enduring and undying belief in God was established. This belief, however, is unfounded. The Aztecs mistakenly believed God had returned when Cortés visited them in 1519, as did the Hawaiians when Capt. James Cook appeared in 1779. The reality is no God exists and no one will ever come to save us. We must, therefore, choose to save ourselves.

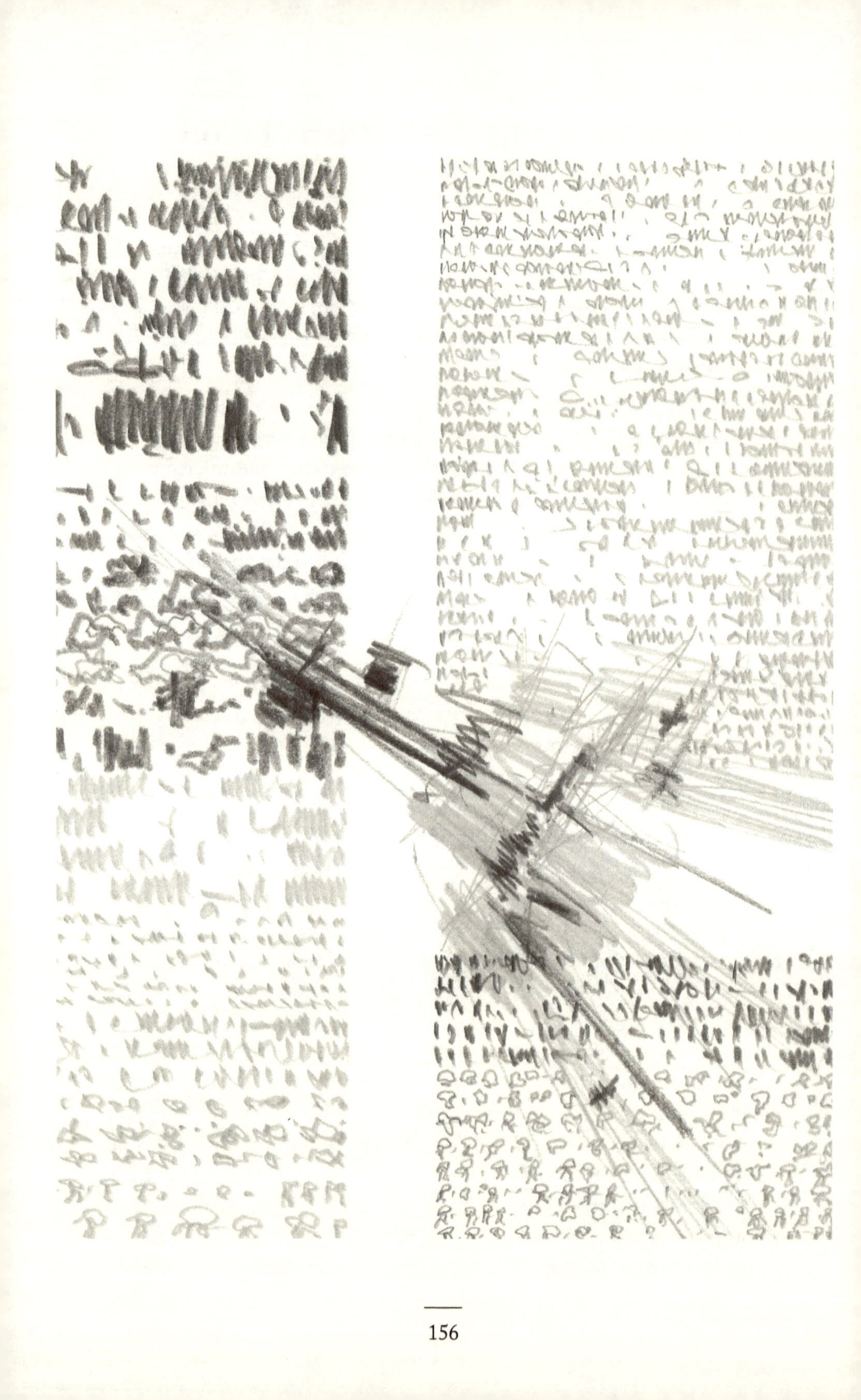

Human Limitations

We were purposefully limited by the ancients.

The ancients had purposefully limited Adam's genetics so his descendants would not be gifted with psionic abilities or long life. They caged the human mind by placing a gatekeeper curse within to restrict access to 10 per cent so to block psionic abilities. They also shortened the human lifespan so to quicken our regenerative ability. This accelerated our internal evolutionary processes, which enabled Adam's descendants, the early humans, to progress and evolve faster than otherwise would be possible.

Our human condition still needs further time to mature and be able to transcend its primitive state. We are yet to quell all that drives us with our selfish **desires** and wants. We quarrel incessantly rather than seek forgiveness or consensus for the common good. Our wants gear us to strive, persist, and endure despite costs. When we fight, we do so to win and succeed, without care of consequences.

Our human condition has been governed by the gatekeeper curse the ancients placed deep in our minds. Dispelling this and gaining complete access will no doubt expand our consciousness, increase our intelligence, and gift us psionic abilities.

To dispel the curse we have within, we must first learn to venture deep into our minds. There, we will need courage to break through and traverse past the many impermeable barriers that include the horrible diseases of schizophrenia and mental illnesses, before battling to overcome and dispel the mind-limiting curse with its gatekeeper. When we succeed and gain full access to our minds, there we will find dormant psionic abilities which we can then wield to reset our genetics so to regain the longevity that already exists within our DNA. We then also will be able to retrieve and reinstate all the gifts bestowed on Adam by the ancients.

The Limited Lifespan

The ancients had manipulated every part of our genetics and physiology. They had purposefully accelerated everything within us so to improve our regenerative ability, but by doing so, they had also shortened our lifespan. They had done this to all who came after Adam, whose **lifespan** they reduce tenfold, limited to one hundred years.

The Mayans sensed this, knowing that humans had an out of sync relationship and affinity with this world, and all that occurs. This they then quantified within their supplementary calendar round which accounted for this human anomaly and inconsistency.

To align to the universal beat, the human lifespan requires two contrasting cycles of counts. The first has a 260-day count, known as the Tzolkin or Tzolk'in, and the second has a 365-day vague solar year count known as the Haab'. When combined, together, the resulting cycle repeats every 52 Haab' or 52 years, signifying half a human lifetime lived.

The ancients' manipulation which had quickened our internal processes had also dialled down the governing number of our physiology, reducing it from Adam's original nine to three. Three being our determining and ruling number, limiting us to three minutes without oxygen, three days without water, and three weeks without food. Imagine if this trebled and was increased to nine?

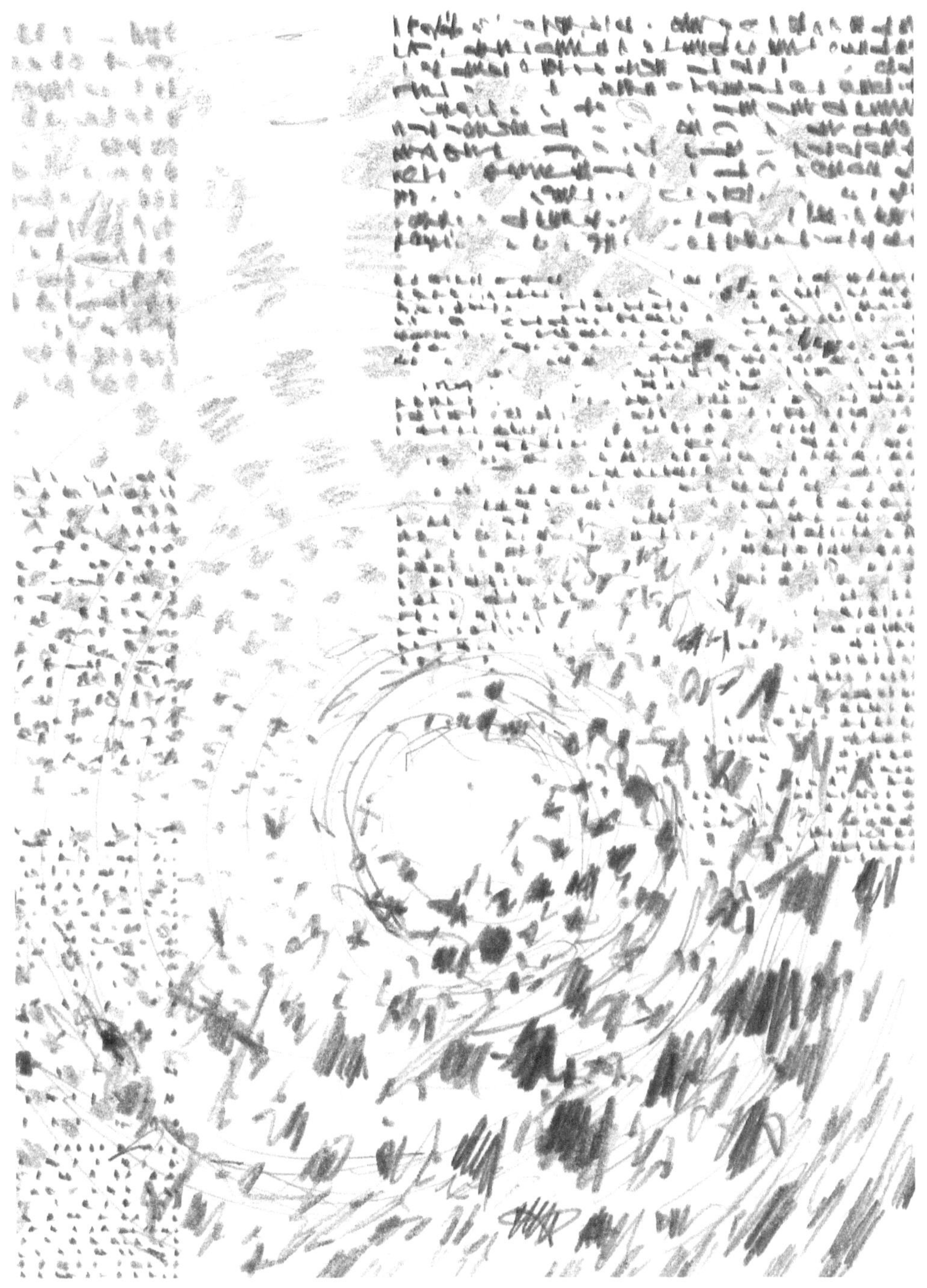

THE ANCIENTS' LINK WITH HUMANITY

Life on Earth evolved as it persisted through numerous destructive yet transformative events and cycles. Some caused mass extinctions that then reset life. Species that did not perish were given the opportunity to adapt, change, evolve, and **transform**.

This is what Earth had willed to happen. It begun destructive cycles so to extinguish life from its surface. Its supercontinent cycle and climatic extremes pushed life to its limits, forced life to recast itself, transform, enhance, and gain resilience merely to persist, endure, and progress.

At first, it had taken an eternity before life sufficiently matured and gained intellect. The most successful were the ancients. They used their abilities to persist, thrive, and then dominate, while others perished. They were not the first but were the most capable and enduring and eventually became the most evolved with enhanced minds and gifted psionic abilities. This, they had naturally acquired, which meant it took another eternity to attain that also took them close to the end of their evolutionary journey. When they realised this, they then sought to find means to gain immortality, which they eventually found within the DNA of the AMH.

We are unlike the ancients as our journey differs. We are a forced evolutionary outcome. We evolved because the ancients had manipulated our genes. They had fast-tracked our progress, bypassing millions of years of otherwise necessary evolutionary time. With this, we gained superior intellect before our time and while we had still a primitive nature. The ancients then placed limits on this gift and governed our minds. We still think we are intelligent as we can manipulate matter, but unlike the ancients, we use our hands, not our minds, and we cannot manipulate space or time. Nor can we stop or halt the quickening that brought us here; as this continues, it has gathered pace and is taking our lineage rapidly to its end before our time.

The Many Forms of the Ancients

The ancients' lineage is more than 250 Ma old. They descended from a reptoid-dinosaur lineage that has since devolved into time. Fortunately for the ancients, they were able to transcend past their mortality and become immortals. They now live in their out-of-phase realm, which exists outside space and time. They achieved this with their psionic abilities, which enabled them to manipulate space, time, and matter and gain immortality. As immortal beings, they now have the means to access anywhere and everywhere and have the power to do anything.

Time and evolution had gifted them their intellect and then their psionic abilities. This then gave them the means to transcend their mortal state and synthesise their bodies so to gain immortality. With this, they also gained the ability to change form, change how they appear, either by retaining or discarding certain body features and characteristics. Their most stable form is the recently adopted mammalian form, making them appear humanoid.

The ancients had gained their form from Adam. Adam was the first, who was gifted with unlimited psionic abilities. He could bring all to yield at will. This, however, the ancients had limited before Adam left Eden so to ensure his descendants did not have full access to their mental or psionic abilities. This was purposefully done so the ancients could maintain control and rule humans on Earth.

When the ancients eventually came to Earth, they came in their original form to establish and secure their kingdom. Humans saw them as dragons, snake-men, and feathered serpents and thought these to be gods, demons, or devils.

History recorded them as the Bellatricians, Saurians, **Anunnaki**, and Mayan gods. Time then enabled the ancients to transform themselves with human DNA, gaining a humanoid form. We now know them as greys or extra-terrestrial aliens, who are occasionally seen when they visit Earth. When they come, they do so to continue with their DNA harvesting.

The Ancient Gods

Why do we fear God?

The ancients were once mortal, like us. Then an eternity of time transformed them, first gifting them superior intellect and then psionic abilities. With these, they gained the means to manipulate all there was, including life. But when time turned against them and began devolving them, they then focused on one simple quest: to gain immortality.

From this quest emerged Adam, an enduring, resilient form that had the genetics the ancients could use to upgrade themselves. They, however, had to wait for Adam's descendants to populate the Earth so to ensure there were sufficient harvestable stocks of DNA. To facilitate this, the ancients helped Adam establish his realm on Earth so his descendants could thrive and survive what was to come.

This was timed with last glacial maximum which began 115,000 years ago. Lowered sea level and connected landmasses enable worldwide **migration**. Pathways were opened to all of Earth's continents. Then when the climate eventually warmed and sea levels rose, populations became landlocked and could no longer move freely. The ancients then called on Adam's surviving descendants to introduce agriculture, religion, and laws to landlocked human populations. Once civilisation established with domesticated life, then the ancients began harvesting. This was when gods appeared reptilian, which they progressively changed as they transformed themselves to mammalian. This enabled them to discard their scales, their multi-coloured feathered skin, and become more humanlike.

A pantheon of gods progressively came and went. Each was different in appearance but all had the same role. Each, in turn, ruled and controlled human society and life. This, they did as they also harvested human DNA so to complete their upgrade. To normalise this came religious sacrificial offerings so to avoid God's wrath. After the harvest, these ceremonies became symbolic and are, what still exist in religion today.

The Greys

The greys are undoubtedly extra-terrestrial beings. We commonly know them as aliens as many believe they are not from Earth. Also, they are readily associated with UFOs and abductions despite this remaining unsubstantiated and unproven.

What is known is that the greys vary in height from 1.2 to 2.1 metres. They all appear the same, with a basic delicate body build which supports an enlarged hairless, smooth dome head. They have noticeably large dark, gleaming reptilian-like, almond-shaped eyes with a sharp gaze. Their facial features are minimal, having small slits for their nose, mouth, and ears. Their arms, hands, and fingers are long and dexterous. Apart from these, they don't have any other appendages, including genitals. Their external skin is like a space suit – smooth, grey, and self-healing. They can easily change their appearance to reptilian or become invisible by making their skin translucent.

The greys, however, are the ancients, originally from Earth. They have always been with us, although in different forms. What is seen is their current synthesised form, which is a result of their transformation from reptilian to mammalian.

This, they had purposefully **engineered** so to enhance their psionic abilities and maintain their immortality. Their body has been designed as an inbuilt resonance that is synced with their mind, which, in turn, magnifies their psionic abilities.

This, their synthesised body, they need to regularly maintain and upkeep so to prevent time devolving their genetics and form. We have become an integral part in enabling this for the ancients. The DNA they source and use for their upkeep is human.

The ancients had placed us here so to provide them with a readily available supply of harvestable, regenerative DNA. This, they now harvest stealthily. They keep their presence and intentions secret by continually erasing all our memories of them with their psionic abilities.

The Anunnaki

On Adam's exit from Eden, the ancients helped his kin establish the first civilisation on Earth. The ancients returned when this ended with the Younger Dryas. They had come to re-establish their kingdom, their dynasty and rule on Earth. History recorded them as the Anunnaki, who ruled the Akkadians, Assyrians, and Babylonians.

Folklore has the original gods An and Ki first visiting Earth to set the fate of humanity by decree. The 'An' part of the name translates to 'the god of the sky', and 'Ki' means the 'princely offspring' or 'offspring of An'. From these gods descended the Anunnaki, who then appointed Adam's direct descendant to help them with their rule, giving them authority with privileges that would be passed down generations and become an **enduring** legacy.

The Anunnaki's reptilian form progressively changed with time, which slowly transformed to look humanoid. They had come to Earth to create a second Garden of Eden, a prison that would house the human population, their harvestable stocks of DNA. To hide this awful truth and their manipulations, they established religion and God worshipping, which required regular sacrificial offerings, which became the ritual shedding of human blood by sacrificing people.

Eventually, the Anunnaki completed their work and returned to their out-of-phase realm. They then elevated Adam's descendants to rulers of the lands, making them the pharaohs and kings. This became our eternal history of enslavement, being unjustly ruled and subjugated with manipulated pain. This has since forged the human psyche, making us who we have become. We all carry repressed memories of subservient feelings that often manifest within. We are unable to explain or reconcile them, as often these fill us with a rage that cannot be dispelled, suppressed, or repressed. This is the ancients' enduring legacy, the pain they had inflicted on us, which time has trapped within our minds, as we cannot remember, but feel.

Early Interventions

Abraham, being the direct descendent of Noah, lived at a time when society was drifting towards gross debauchery. God saved him with the promise that his descendants would be as 'numerous as the stars in the sky and as countless as the sand on the seashore'. This promise was made at the end of Abraham's life, when he was still childless, aged in his late eighties. The ancients easily fulfilled their promise, they simply extended what they had previously reduced; the human lifespan, and used their genetic reserves to seed Abraham's wife. Abraham then had his first son at eighty-nine and his last at a hundred years old, but instead of bringing hope to a suffering people and world, Abraham's descendants became the chosen few, inheriting privileges and status that enabled them to rule and subjugate their people. This was God's will. God had given Abraham His seed to produce His children, who were given His reserved privileges.

The ancients did this as the debauchery that occurred had begun to corrupt the human DNA and they needed to recast it so to suit their needs. With this, they again gained control of human genetics.

With Abraham, God then stopped all human sacrifices and the ritual shedding of **sacred** human blood. Animals became the sacrificial substitutes, which continued, so to remind believers, of the penalty of loss of innocence with sin. To reinforce this, God later voluntarily sacrificed his son Jesus, who shed his blood as 'the lamb of God who took away the sin of this world'.

God had similarly used Moses to do His bidding, when tasked with leading the enslaved to a promised distant land. God did this so to re-structure society with new laws and rules. This was how the ancients manipulated the unfortunate, who then simply exchanged one ruler for another, albeit the latter being the almighty. Such manipulation of human affairs has continued to the present day by way of sacred messages. The latest is the Qur'an, which God send to guide our development along His path, with help from the chosen ones, the descendants of Adam.

Creation and Yahweh

Why did the Jewish calendar set creation date 5,784 years ago?

The Jewish faith set its creation date when God made this world real for the Israelites. This was when humans supposably manifested into existence by the will of God. This date was based on rabbinic calculations, the Masoretic text, and the Greek Septuagint, which set creation at 3,761 BC. The Mayans differed, setting creation later at 11 August 3,114 BC, which then became part of their long count calendar. Other cultures and religions based this on Adam's birthdate. The oldest calculation was made in AD 412 by Panodorus, an Alexandrian monk, which set Adam's birth date at 5,904 BC, 7927 years ago. The next oldest was recorded by the Byzantine calendar, set at 5,509 BC.

Despite the differences, creation date established an important **baseline** and precedent. It did not mark Adam's birth date, rather, it marked when greater humanity awoke, and gained full awareness with intellect. This occurred after Adam's descendants had already established civilisation and ruled on Earth for 117,000 years.

Our creation date was set after the Younger Dryas, when religion and God worshipping were needed to rule of the lesser evolved and unruly humans. This spread worldwide, to all people, which enabled the ancients to become the original Canaanite gods and goddesses, who eventually emerged to become the one true creator God, Yahweh, the storm-and-warrior god who would then forevermore rule this world and universe. Soon after, Yahweh became faceless and nameless as He represented the community of the ancients. He was not benevolent, rather He sought to have subjects to control and manipulate.

Yahweh selected the Israelites, whom He then helped and protected. He appointed priests, whom He used to end their Babylonian captivity period, and guide the Israelites to a religious life. This however, was the ancients' next manipulated closed breeding program, so they could attain and source the genetics they needed.

The Faceless and Nameless God

The Younger Dryas had forced Adam's surviving descendants to combine and collaborate with the lesser evolved AMHs. Their intellect and knowledge made them natural rulers. The knowledge they imparted introduced agriculture, civilisation, religion, class, and the rule of law. With these, communities were established that tie people to places.

The ancients had planned this. They wanted the human population to quickly homogenise. As this occurred, the ancients returned as gods to rule. First, they ruled by decree and then with religion. They did this to prepare humans for their harvest. They had waited millions of years for this moment. They needed substantial amounts of human genetics to transform their entire colony into mammalian. To achieve this and avoid dissention or rebellion, they then tied everything to religion with sacrificial and sacred rituals.

From this emerged Yahweh, the proclaimed true creator God. This marked the start the Abrahamic religions, which occurred when the Second Temple was built in **Jerusalem**. Priests then used religious ceremonies to entrenched beliefs while dispelling rival gods. These priests then ensured everything associated with Yahweh became sacred, including His name and image. They would not speak His name or show His image. They did this to ensure Yahweh became a faceless and nameless God, named thereafter simply 'Adonai' or 'my Lord'.

Being faceless and nameless amplified His reverence. This also elevated the significance and status of His priests, who held His sacred knowledge. This secrecy ensured God's rule could never be questioned – and nor would there be any further explanations.

Soon, what was inscribed in stone on temples became scripture. The oldest in use is the Tanakh, written in 450 BC, while the newest is the Qur'an, written in AD 632. Both are different and yet the same, as both carry the same message; telling humans how to live and obey God's rules.

Mayan Gods

The gods that ruled Earth appeared soon after the Younger Dryas. Many appeared **simultaneously**, globally, in countries such as Mesopotamia, Cambodia, Egypt, the Indus Valley, China, and Central America. At each location then sprang civilisation with a religion that subjugated people to its rule.

Quetzalcóatl was one of many important gods who appeared to the Mayans in Central America, the Yucatán Peninsula region. Quetzalcóatl was also known as Kukulkan, a part-reptoid being who was a revered and worshipped god. This god was seen by the Mayans as a **feathered serpent**, whose image was placed on all important temples and buildings. Another equally well-known and important Mayan god was Itzamna, whose name meant 'lizard house'. It was written that he was the direct descendant of the creator gods: the original god Hunab Ku, the sun god Kinich Ahau, and the goddess Ix Chel.

These gods, as others, were not benevolent. They had come demanding payment by way of human sacrifices and ritual offerings. To achieve this, they brought their appointed priests, the surviving descendants of Adam, who then forced people into lives of servitude, with ritual sacrificial offerings. They also improved the lives of the Mayan. The sacred knowledge they imparted enabled the Mayans to cultivate corn, write, prepare medicine, and record time. With this, the Mayan numbers grew, communities became cities, and civilisation commenced. As this occurred, the priests ensured the ancients' strict rules were always followed when making offerings. Each was a ritual that required substantial preparation. Each was structured to please, appease, and feed these gods. What was offered included special maize bread, maize, cacao drinks, honey liquor, flowers, incense nodules, rubber figures, cigars, and people.

The Mayan Long Count Calendar

The gods had gifted the Mayans their sacred long count calendar. This calendar broadened the Mayans' thinking as it provided an informed view of history. It also revealed to the Mayans the long continuity of time and the cyclical nature of life. This calendar was so revered that it was adopted by each subsequent dynasty of the Yucatan region, including the Mixtecs, the Aztecs, and most recently, the people in the Guatemalan highlands, who still use this same calendar.

The long count calendar has captured the

universal pulse.

It provides a way to measure what occurs in this world and universe. The longer measures are used to set the ages of planets, solar systems, and creation while the shorter measures are used to mark key formation events, such as mass extinctions.

The day 21 December 2012 was the most recent calendar round anniversary. This marked the thirteenth of twenty *b'ak'tun*, an insignificant event, being a small part of a much longer count.

On 13 October 4772, the *b'ak'tun* series will end, and the *piktun* cycle, being 7,885 years long, will commence. In the year AD 154,590, twenty *piktun*s would have passed, triggering the commencement of the *kalabtun* cycle. After twenty *kalabtun*, 3,154,071 years would have passed, which will then commence the *k'inchiltun* series. After twenty *k'inchiltun*, 63,081,429 years would have passed, taking us to AD 63,078,315. This is when the last series, the *alautun*, commences, and this universe will reach the ripe age of 219 *alautun*, possibly also marking the date when the next dominant species will awaken on Earth.

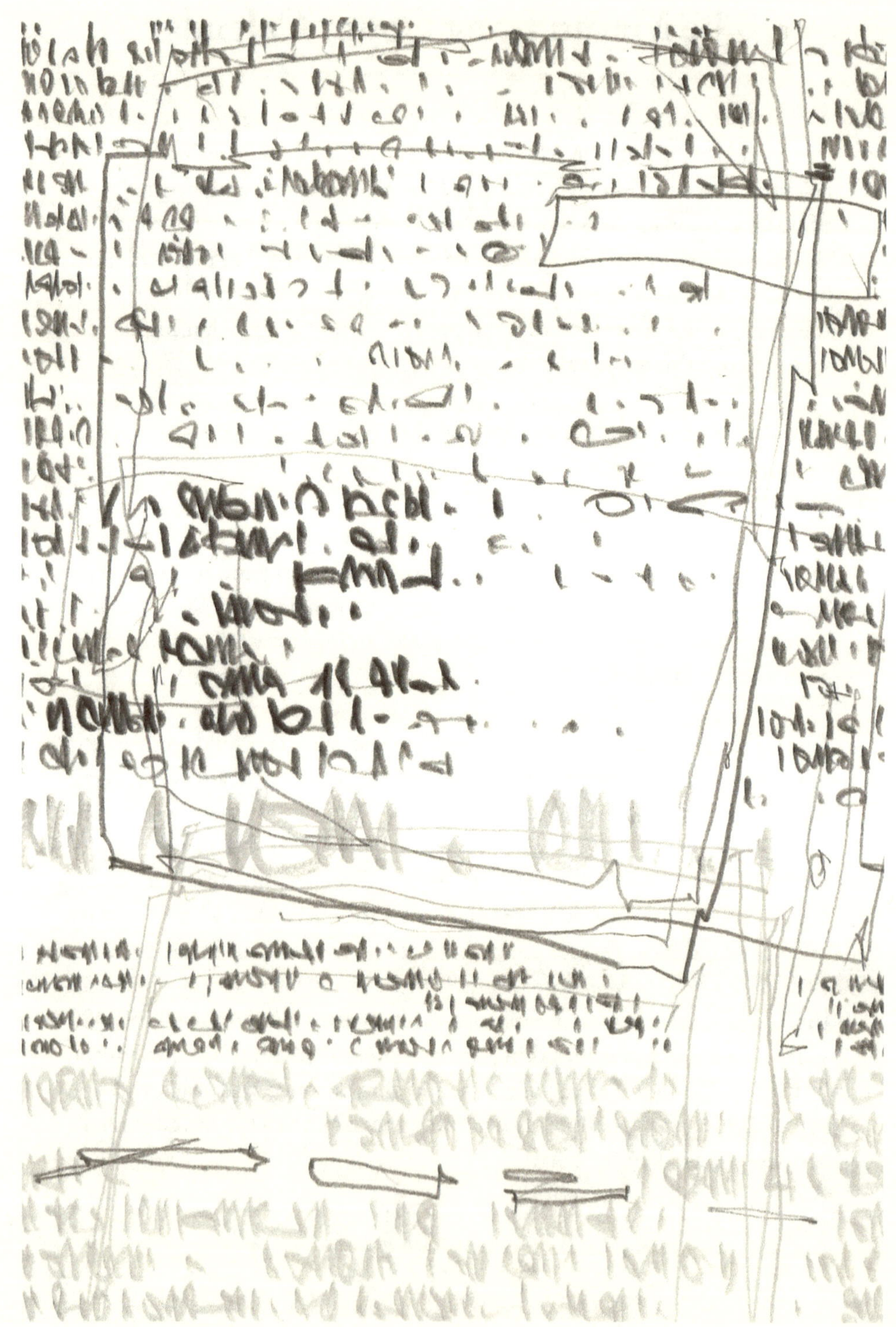

The Mayan Long Count of Measures

Mayan Measure	Time in years from Mayan Creation Day	Event
–218 alautun	–13.8 Ga	The big bang – the birth of the universe.
–206 alautun	–13 Ga	The birth of the Milky Way.
–72 alautun	–4.5 Ga	The birth of this solar system and Earth forms.
–60 alautun	–3.7 Ga	The birth of LUCA, the ancestor of all life on Earth.
–10 alautun	–630 Ma	The Precambrian and Vendian mass extinction.
–7 alautun	–441 Ma	The Ordovician-Silurian mass extinction.
–6 alautun	–378 Ma	The late Devonian mass extinction.
–4 alautun	–252 Ma	The Great Dying; the Permian-Triassic mass extinction.
–3.2 alautun	–201 Ma	The Triassic-Jurassic mass extinction.
–1 alautun	–63 Ma	The Age of Mammals begins after the Cretaceous-Paleogene mass extinction.
–2 k'inchiltun	–6.3 Ma	Hominins appear at the end of the Miocene epoch.
–2 kalabtun	–315,408 years	AMHs appear.
–15 b'ak'tun	–5,910 years	The start of the Holocene epoch within the Quaternary period 9,000 BC.
Creation Date	**Baseline Measure**	**Mayan Creation Day (11 August 3,114 BC)**
+13 b'ak'tun	+5,126 years	Most recent Mayan anniversary event – 21 December 2012 AD.
+1 piktun	+7,886 years	The first *pitkun* – 13 October 4,772 AD.
+1 kalabtun	+160,818 years	The first *kalabtun* after Creation Day.
+1 k'inchiltun	+3.1 Ma	The first *k'inchiltun* after Creation Day
+1 alautun	+63 Ma	The first *alautun* after Creation Day.
+5 alautun	+315 Ma	The next mass extinction with the breakup of supercontinent Amasia.
+1,585 alautun	+100 Ga	The predicted end of the life; all energy sources of this universe will be exhausted.

Table 1. Key milestone events of the long count calendar.

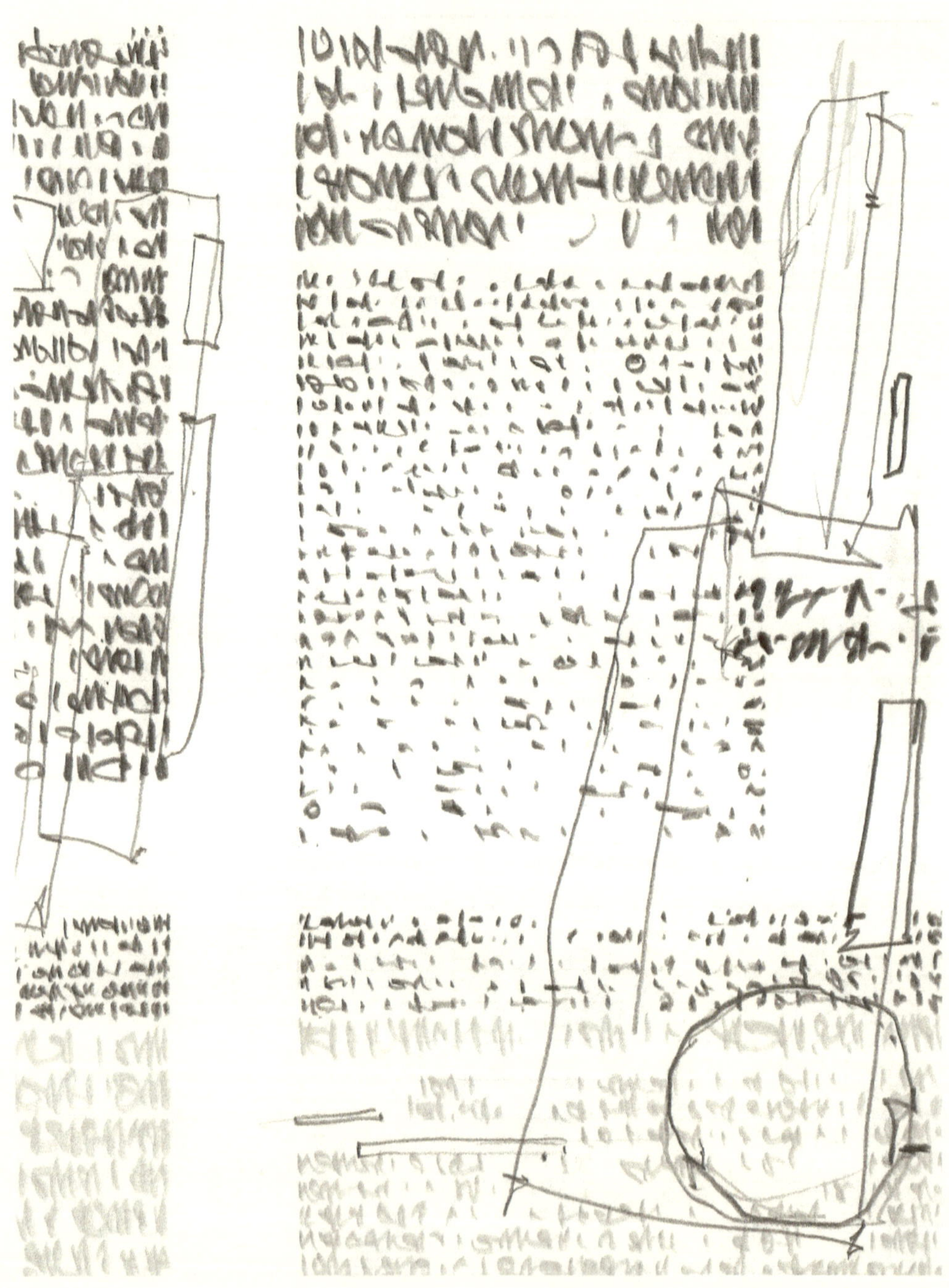

The Long Count

All motion and thereby life in this universe is governed by the universe's pulse with its accompanying slower beat. This pulse sets the time for the beat, which also baselines everything as everything is synchronised to it, including the pace of evolution. On Earth, this beat is felt as years, seasons, days, hours, minutes, and seconds. Despite being ubiquitous, regular, and unending, this beat is incomprehensible as it also sets the destiny for all that exists and occurs.

The Mayans knew this pulse existed along with its slower, differing beat. They also knew this influenced everything, including their lives.

The measure of the pulse began with the big bang, when universal consciousness awoke. For the Mayans, this occurred when they gained understanding and intellect, marking this as their creation date. This gave them the context to understand their place in this universe.

The long count calendar is best understood when it is wound back to its beginning. At one *alautun* ago, the of Age of Mammals began which occurred at the end of the Cretaceous-Paleogene mass extinction. Taken back further and using whole-number *alautun* measures, it becomes apparent that these mark all previous mass extinctions, occurring at three, four, six, and seven *alautun*. Taken further back, at sixty *alautun*, life began on Earth. At 72 *alautun*, Earth formed, and at 218 *alautun*, the big bang occurred.

This *alautun* measure, set at 63 Ma, has recorded the time this universe takes to pulse. All lesser measures are synchronised and tied to this. The second longest measure is the *k'inchiltun* cycle, set at 3 Ma. This series marks significant evolutionary events, such as when the first hominins appeared at two *k'inchiltun* ago. The next measure is the *kalabtun*, set at 157,704 years, which marks the development of species, such as when the AMHs appeared at two *kalabtun* ago. Next is the *piktun*, set at 7,885 years. Two *piktun* ago began the Holocene epoch as Earth's climate stabilised. The next shortest is also the last series, the *b'ak'tun*, set at 394 years. This measure relates to known time, starting with the Mayan Creation Day, set at 13 *b'ak'tun* or 5,136 years ago.

Transcendence of the Gods

Geb was an important Egyptian deity who came from the Great Ennead of Heliopolis. Being the

father of snakes and reptilian

he wielded enormous power. He could determine what lived on Earth. His mere presence brought renewal and enabled life to flourish, while his laughter caused death with earthquakes. Geb was also proclaimed to be the creator god, who enabled the divine goose to lay its egg, which gave birth to Earth.

Geb, however, was only one of the many gods who came to Earth to rule. All had come after the Younger Dryas to claim what was theirs. They all had participated in creating Adam and allowed him to spread his seed on Earth. They had now returned to help establish humanity so they could also reap their harvest, the descendants of Adam.

We all carry within what God gifted Adam. We therefore are indebted to Him. Despite not understanding the significance of or our role in this, we nevertheless subconsciously know. This knowing has manifested as an eternal yearning to be free, freed from both gods and rulers. We know and feel this as we are constantly reminded with the tales, folklore, legends, mythologies, and scriptures that our ancestors wrote to warn us. All reveal an eternal struggle, always being powerless against the pantheon of deities, gods, and even demons, all who wielded some divine authority on Earth. Religion now mirrors this as it continues to tell us how we should be living life on Earth.

The Commencement of Civilisation

The ancients had maintained a close relationship with Adam's descendants of prehistory. They had shown them their technology and advanced society with the impossible structures that existed in their lair. They were told this was God's domain, as creation had occurred there. They also were told this was heaven as it existed outside Earth, space, and time.

After the Younger Dryas, they mandated Adam's surviving descendants with re-establishing civilisation. They did this by encouraging the lesser evolved AMHs to settle with them so to establish communities that they could protect and rule. When labour became available and abundant, they then began replicating God's kingdom on Earth, rebuilding what they had previously achieved before the Younger Dryas.

As this occurred, the ancients took many of the lesser evolved humans back to their lair for reprogramming, indoctrination, and further genetic manipulation. Not all survived. Those that did told of a fantastical journey, which became the tales of the

underworld and heavens that have persisted to this day.

Few who had returned were gifted with sacred knowledge and special abilities. These survivors then gained prominence with authority. Some were even elevated to become the new rulers, only to be then tasked with enacting God's will on Earth. The less fortunate were the majority. These were the people who could not be indoctrinated. When released, they suffered, as the ancients tracked and monitored them, causing them to fear recapture. This fear had since morphed into an anger that has tied itself to the human psyche. This now lingers within us all, which has since manifested as the endless conflicts and wars that have accompanied us through this modern time.

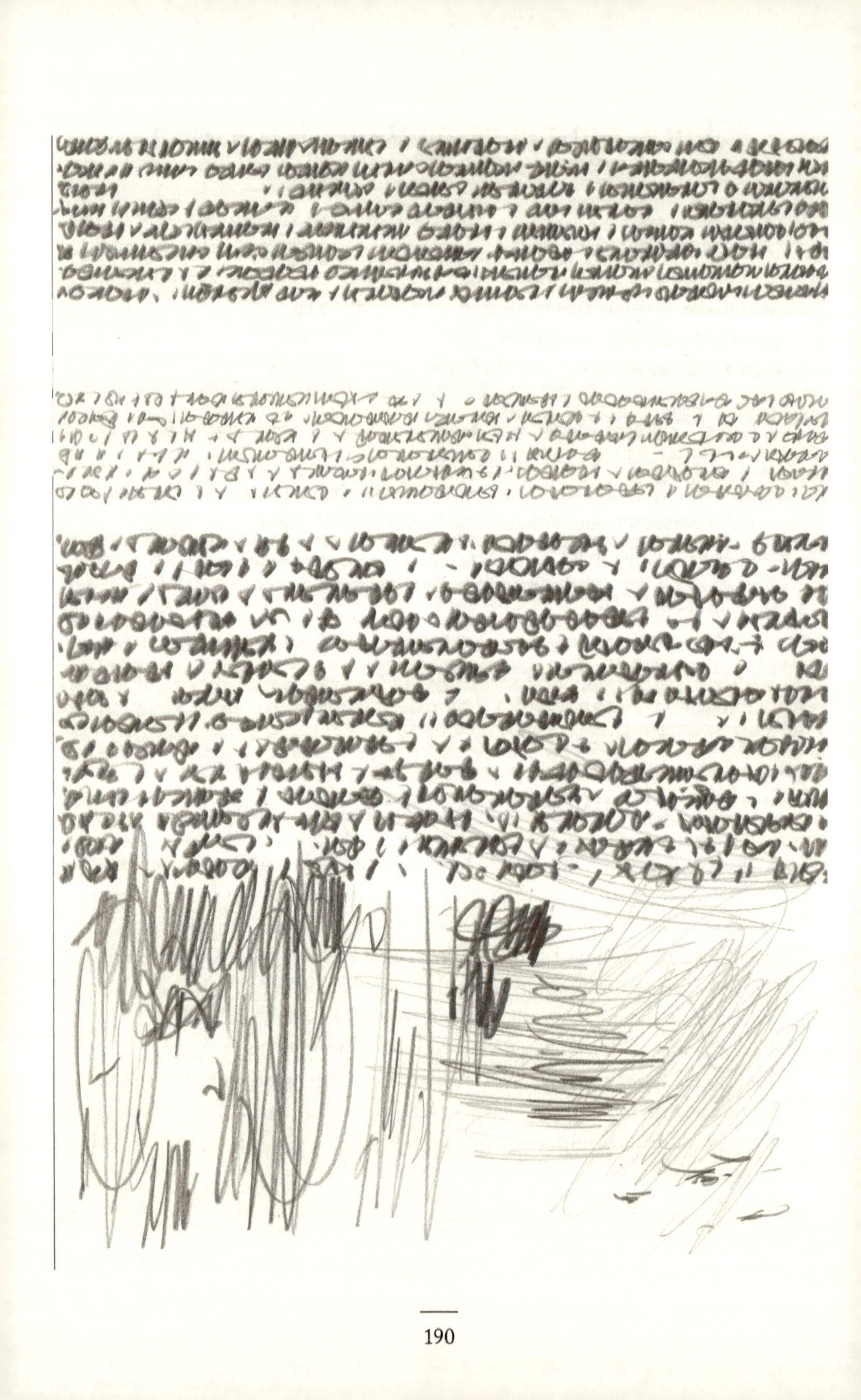

The Pyramids

Before the Younger Dryas, Adam's descendants had already replicated God's kingdom on Earth. They achieved this in prehistory with help from the ancients, who had gifted some of them psionic abilities to enable this.

The **architecture** they built, however, was destroyed by the Younger Dryas. All that remained when civilisation recommenced were memories. One which lingered was the pyramid form. This was an interpretation of what was seen in the ancients' lair. This form, with its shape, was thought to enable mere mortals to reconnect with the gods and even attain psionic power.

From this belief began a worldwide building program, with pyramids appearing in Mesopotamia, Egypt, the Indus Valley, China, and Mexico. All were built with the belief that these would entice the ancients to return. However, when this did not occur, this then expanded to include sacrificial rituals, replicating what the ancients had previously done to humans. It was believed, combining both the pyramid form with sacrificial rituals would provide a direct pathway to the gods.

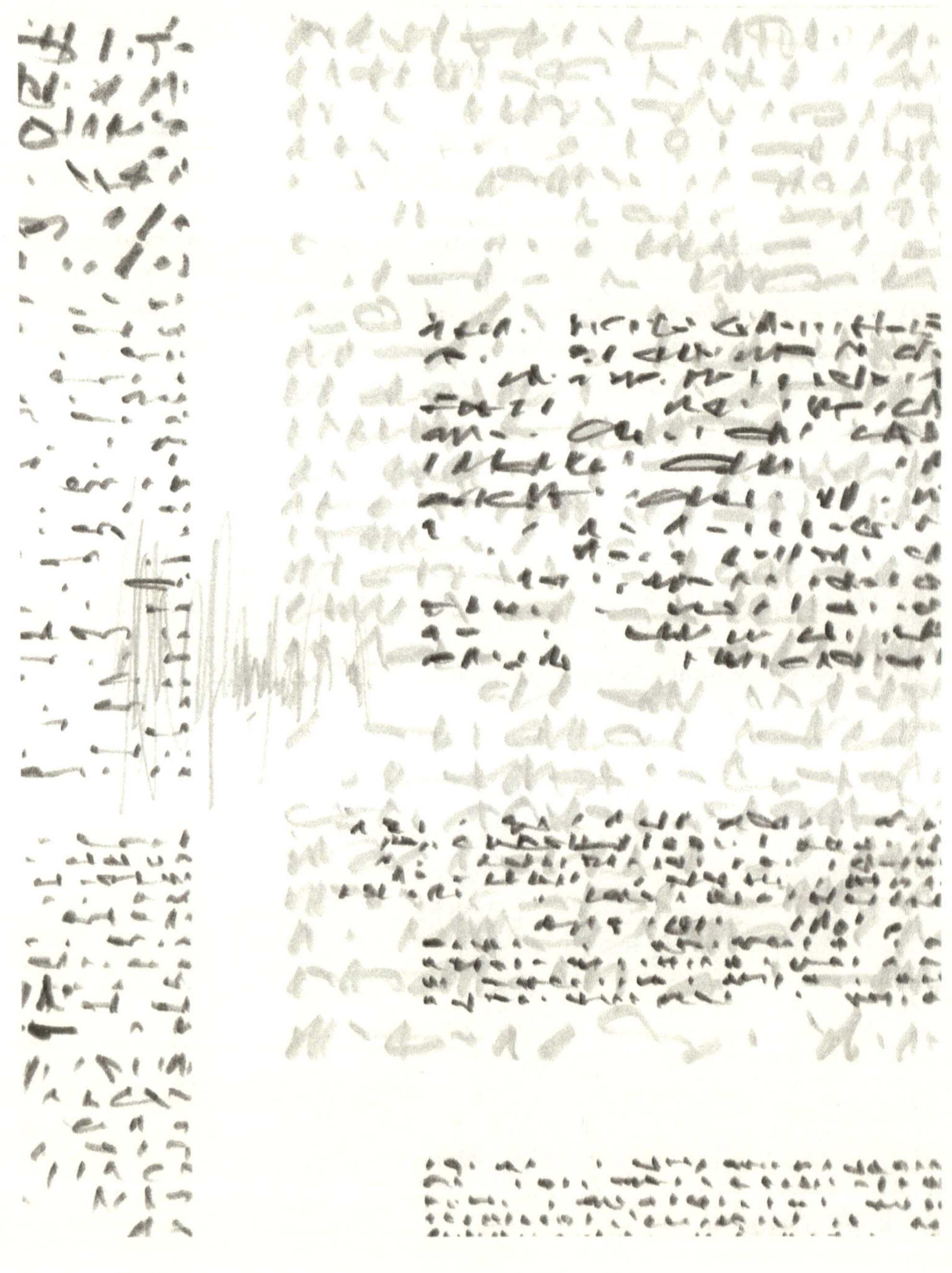

The Continuance of the Ancients' Legacy

The time is coming, declares the Lord, when God will put laws in minds and write them on hearts. (Hebrews 8:8–10)

The ancients used religion to sway the human spirit and mind. This began with sacred ceremonies, teachings, and scriptures, which ritualised lives, influenced beliefs, and directed thinking. These then became God's laws and rules, which ensured **obedience**.

The belief that a Messiah will soon come and deliver us from evil, and at death, if we submit will take us to God's Kingdom of Glory, is ingrained in society, persisting to this date. Deep down, however, we know this will not happen. We are not the chosen ones, and nor will we be saved. Death will become us, as we are mere mortals, destined to die.

Only the ancients can set and determine our fate. They are the true masters of Earth and heaven. They are the immortal beings, the gods who wield divine power and have the means to create or destroy all that exists. They were here before us and will continue to exist long after us.

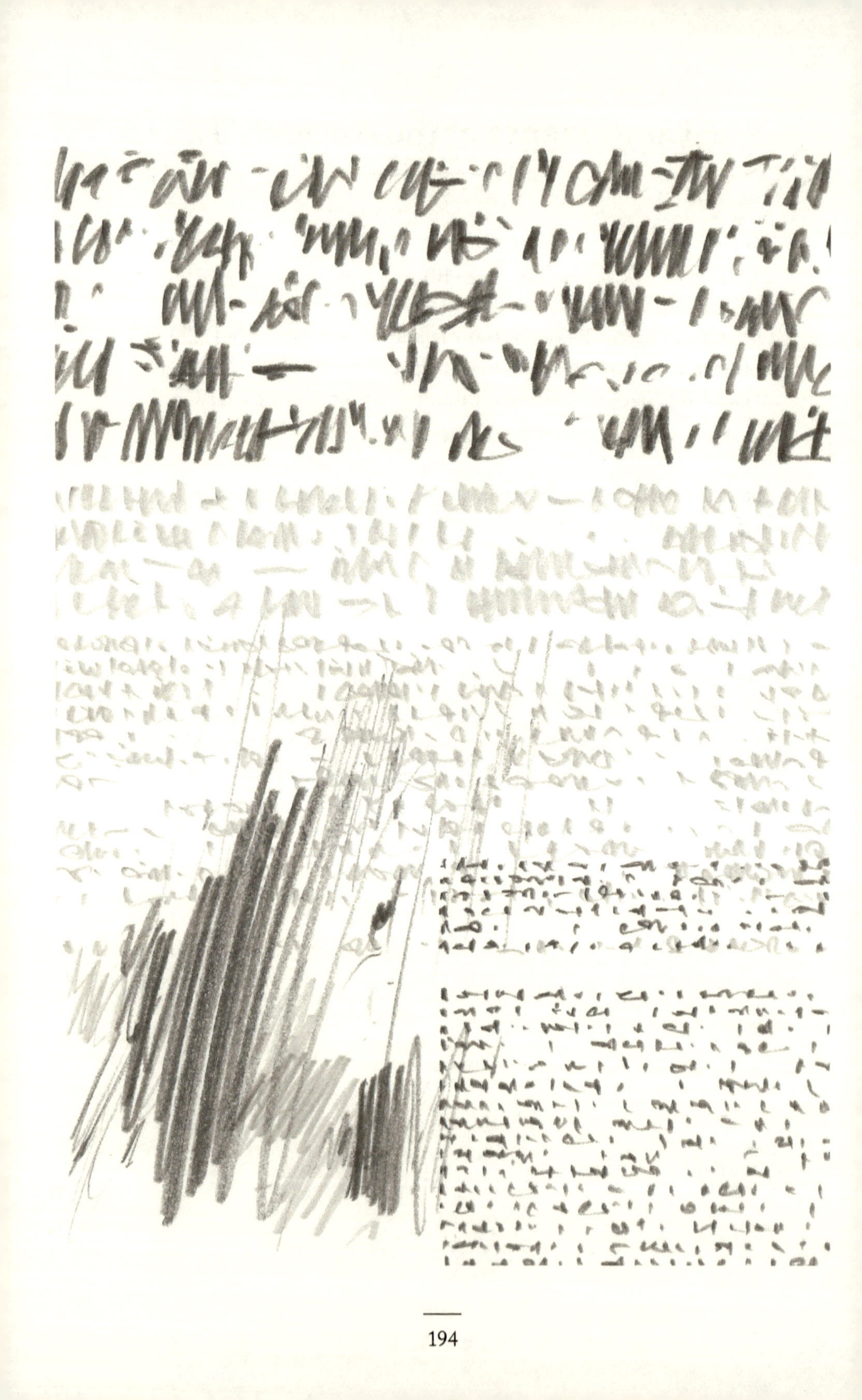

The Sacrificed

Why did our ancestors sacrifice their kin?

Was this done to appease some angry god?

Are sacrificial rituals merely copying what the ancients do?

Humans are the ancients' harvestable stock of DNA, which they now use to upkeep their synthesised form. Rarely, they find new mutated genetics which can be used to further upgrade themselves. When they do find this, they then literally sacrifice these individuals, not so to appease the gods but rather to retain and further experiment on their DNA.

In our midst are the ancients' agents, the chosen ones. These are the nobility and ruling classes on Earth: Adam's direct descendants. Most, however, have lost their way, forgotten their real purpose and reason for their existence. Nevertheless, they continue to rule as they are unwilling to relinquish or share any power or authority.

The ancients placed them there long ago to control us. They tasked them with keeping populations occupied and divided so to subjugate all into servitude. There, these agents wait for God's return while wielding their power and instilling fear en masse.

Through transference, we now all think the same. We all yearn for **God's return**, and we all want to be saved despite not knowing why. This yearning highlights the level of our indoctrination and conditioning. We simply are unable to accept there is no real God or heaven and that none has ever existed or will ever exist. Nor can we accept that no one will save us. We have damned ourselves by not facing this reality as this has corrupted our understanding of how life should be lived here, with one another, on this world.

Alien Abductions

There is no higher aspiration than to be free.

The ancients became gods when they acquired psionic abilities. One mere thought of theirs could overwhelm any lesser being. When the ancients combined their abilities, together, they gain the means to manipulate all that exists, including us.

Why do aliens abduct us?

Remote viewing enables the ancients to see all there is. They know who we are, what we have, where we are, and what we think. When they find suitable individuals, they then target them to abduct. These, they take to their lair to conduct experiments, manipulate their genetics, and at times extract parts of their DNA. When finished, they wipe their minds before they release these victims, so nothing is remembered. I experienced this when abducted. I remember feeling their overwhelming power with intense, paralysing fear that affected every fibre of my being. This made me succumb to their every wish.

The ancients' earliest experimentations on stem mammals begun 221 Ma ago. As they progressed this lifeform, the first mammals emerged, followed by primates and then the AMH. They then progressively upgraded the AMH with many implants that included their seed. This fast tracked the evolutionary process, bypassing hundreds of millions of years of otherwise necessary time.

What the ancients had done to us, they have also done to many other species in other worlds. With their manipulations, they have established a large range of compatible sources to harvest. We are now one small part of this growing **network** of related intelligent life that exists in this universe. The most similar are the star people. They look like us but are superior in all respects except that their minds can be occupied. The ancients have used this race as avatars to progress their search for evolved genetics while also continuing to seed life on many other worlds. This, the ancients will continue to do until they find an eternal synthesised form.

Saving the Planet

The ancients have no desire or need to dominate or wage war. They already are all-powerful and can decimate any lesser being at will. A single thought of theirs carries the power to create or destroy as they wield godlike, divine powers.

The ancients have chosen to remain hidden from our modern life. They have ensured no historical record exists of their presence. They have done this despite having always previously accompanied us on our long evolutionary journey. Despite us not seeing them, they are close by, and within society, they have their agents. These are the people tasked with enacting their will on Earth. These people are in charge; they rule us by dictating to authorities how to subjugate and control all we do.

The ancients often help their agents by manipulating the minds of the general public. They do this by linking with our random thoughts, which they then merge with implanted suggestions and ideas. These then either realign or changes what we think. They do this remotely, stealthily, without our knowing. All we sense are

thought messages, believing these are ours.

The ancients have also continued to impart their sacred knowledge to us. They do this to provide new insight and opportunities. The most recent were related to digital, healing, and anti-polluting technologies. With these, we are able to embrace greater environmental concerns, which then limited the harm we caused this planet. The ancients continue to do this as they fear our warmongering technologies may yet dominate and lead us to some end, which may then extinguish life on Earth.

POST HUMAN

All there ever was and is has previously occurred.

Today our future seems closer than our past. This is because the repetitive cycle of life has accelerated. A quickening has occurred that has increased the pace of our lives and is taking us rapidly to some destiny. This, we all feel but cannot explain, quantify, or understand. We can only sense this, perceiving shortened hours, days, weeks, months, and years despite an unchanged time beat.

Everything seems to pass quickly by. Change is constant. New realities rapidly emerge, all with shortened durations. Everything that had previously existed seems to quickly fade as past paradigms change and end all that was familiar. The present seems already distant and old as the unstoppable pace of new breakthroughs and interactions occur. This quickening is rapidly closing past falsehoods while establishing new, with their own truths and reality. This has created a transitional time, forcing all to wait for an event destined to come, promising to release us from this stagnant reality.

We are yet to fully understand or **reconcile** all that has occurred and is occurring. The blur of the recent rapid events has fogged our minds and dampened our ability to think rationally or clearly. Society seems hindered and paralysed with inaction, failing to comprehend or appreciate its present dilemma. This has limited our awareness of the transcendence that has started, as the repetitive cycle of life is forcing its change on us, takes us to its new future.

Many important choices are already with us to make. And what we decide may potentially determine whether we progress or perish as a race. Presently, we just seem to endure to persist, while we oscillate between a conflicted past and present. We must use all our intellect and might and unite as a race, as a global community, link our minds, so together, we can emerge, become one that will be able to transcend its present and transition into a new post-human state.

Human Intelligence and Psionic Abilities

If humanity is lucky to persist for hundreds of millions of years, it will surely change, possibly merge into one being, and become part of the greater consciousness. When this occurs, all that humanity has achieved, what it has built (its buildings, infrastructure, and cities), and all that it had known (with its different tongues, languages, cultures, states, countries, and arbitrary borders) will all end and vanish. What will remain will be our essence and intelligence, together with our minds and consciousness, and if our minds do evolve and are able to merge, then we will likely also gain the ancients' abilities and powers.

We, however, are not like the ancients. We are still primitive, having only begun our evolutionary journey. As *Homo sapiens*, we have only existed for 315,000 years, an insignificantly short amount of time. We therefore are still evolving and yet to attain full use of our minds and our abilities.

Intelligence is the enabler, a precursor for attaining psionic abilities. It purposefully prolongs the evolutionary processes so to delay access to such powers. Species must first transcend past some evolutionary threshold to be gifted such abilities as these, they will find, wield the most powerful force in this universe. With it comes also a transcendence that enables species to exit the cycle of life and gain immortality.

The ancients attained this. This had enabled them to force evolution, transforming them into immortal superbeings. With their abilities and wisdom, they then created Adam, gifted with comparable abilities, having both superior intellect and psionic abilities. This, however, the ancients then purposefully limited so not pass these to Adam's descendants and so these would not be used to define humanity. Remnants of these, however, still exist within us all, albeit deeply suppressed within.

To reach a post-human state, we must first break free from our past and the ancients' hold. With this, we will gain full access of our minds and abilities that will enable us to fulfil our destiny.

The Einstein Principle

History has recorded many examples of individuals doing extraordinary and impossible things. These are the individuals that have traversed through many limiting barriers placed by the ancients in our minds. There, they gained access to parts of the ubiquitous, sacred knowledge with universal truths that have long existed within us.

Einstein was one such rare individual. He had managed to briefly unlock the forbidden parts of his mind. This expanded his understanding and mind capacity, albeit only by an incremental 3 per cent above the norm. This slight increase, however, gave him the ability to decipher otherwise incomprehensible concepts and ideas. We all have this potential. We all have this within us, but only few can access these otherwise forbidden parts of our minds. This is where the sacred knowledge lies, yet it is still well beyond our grasp. The ancients had purposefully locked this so to **limit** us. At the entrance of these locked chambers, they placed a gatekeeper, to stop us venturing further within. When a certain threshold is traversed, gatekeeper, for most, will inflict pain and harm that will overwhelm and then corrupt the mind with mental illness and the disease of schizophrenia.

We need more time to evolve and mature before we can tackle and overcome this gatekeeper. We must first transcend our primitive nature, complete with its urges and desires, and then expand our awareness and intellect. This will help us disable and then dispel the gatekeeper, which will then open all the previously dormant and locked parts of our minds. With this, we will gain psionic abilities and access to the ancients' sacred knowledge, which will then surely give us new purpose.

Presently, however, gaining access to such unlimited power would possibly destroy us. We would produce damning technologies and create murderous weapons with ballistics. The hope is that future evolved humans gain sufficient wisdom so when they gain such abilities and knowledge, they use these wisely and appropriately.

The Rise of the Human Consciousness

We may call ourselves modern, but the reality is our condition is still primitive. We have not yet fully evolved. We have not yet mastered our minds. We lack the full use of our intellect. We don't have psionic abilities, and nor can we remote view or communicate telepathically. We are yet to overcome gravity and our mortality. We let our material wants and needs drive us, swaying and ruling our minds, allowing these to corrupt our thoughts with sinful desires and acts. This prevent us from seeing the reality of what is and distinguishing the truth from falsehoods or illusions.

We are both preconditioned and controlled with measures that **divert** our thoughts and prevent us from accepting, recognising, or registering the truth of our reality. We also have an inbuilt, unintentional blindness and inattentiveness that fills our minds with self-absorbed thoughts focused on self-fulfilment and desires. This has allowed the ancients to hide in plain sight. We regularly encounter them, and yet our mind does not register them.

The majority of the 315,000 years of evolutionary time we have had has been marred and constrained by the ancients' preconditioning. We only see and think what the ancients want us to see and think. This, we need to overcome to truly open and free our minds. Only then will we be able to see the truth and realise how strange life really is.

I felt and saw the truth when I entered the ancients' out-of-phase realm. There, all my preconditioning vanished. This is where evolution transcends as this realm's resonance expands awareness, frees minds, so everything is understood. It was there that I learnt what transpired and how stuck our minds are in the past but destined to someday, move beyond its present governed state. This, however, will only occur after we learn to share, collaborate, combine our thoughts, minds, and create one global consciousness. With this, I sensed, we will also gain the means to evolve to our next stage of development, the post-human state.

Pre-Determined Destiny

As immortals, the ancients are the essence of pure intelligence. Their destiny is to someday merge with the one community mind and the greater consciousness. While they wait, they meditate together, focusing their minds so to harness and magnify their power from the singular to the collective. This focused collaboration expands their minds, gifting them access to godlike abilities, enabling them to create and manifest new realities into existence.

The ancients' contemplations have also shown them the likely future. They know all that will likely eventuate. They have seen time unfold in their minds and thereby know what is in store for us humans. This, they monitor so to ensure we remain on the path. They care for us humans as they had made us into what we have become. With this, they also set our destiny as we are, one day, destined to join them in their out-of-phase realm. We must, however, first free ourselves from the illusion of this existence so to attain the certainty that will enable us to transcend past our present state.

We have everything we need within to progress but lack access and time. Our minds are limited and governed by 90 per cent. Limited, we flounder, and without full awareness, we continue with the harm we cause to this world. We are simply unable to fully comprehend the recklessness of our actions or the predicament we have placed ourselves in. We must wait for some evolutionary trigger to open the **unreachable** and sealed parts of our minds. In the meantime, this has damned us and this world.

Eventually, we will gain the awareness we lack and overcome these limitations. We will then be able to link our minds with one another and with the universal consciousness, which will give us access to all the sacred knowledge that exists.

Transcendence

All life on Earth descended from the same single source. We are all genetically related to the first organic life, LUCA. Evolution then diverted as each new species emerged and set their own path. The ancients had manipulated this when it came to the mammalian lifeform, implanting their DNA into this species to upgrade and make them compatible. This accelerated evolution and produced many variant forms. Each version gained greater awareness, and some were gifted with intellect. They did this, needing to produce species with evolved DNA that would provide them with an enduring synthesised form. We became the outcome of this, when our lineage emerged as the most enduring form. This then also tied our fate and destiny with the ancients.

From that time, the ancients governed us. By design, they kept humanity separated and divided so to limit and keep the population disorganised and in a submissive, primitive state, one that could then be ruled.

We are yet to learn the power of **collaboration**. As seen in warfare, individuals and disorganised groups perish easily, while integrated, cohesive groups can significantly magnify their powers, abilities, and strength, greater than the sum of their disparate individuals. This is how the ancients overcame their limitations. They had merged their abilities and united their minds into one. A transcendence then occurred, followed with transformative change that expanded their awareness and enhanced their state of being. This is how we can similarly diminish the impossibilities that face us – by uniting, combining our minds, we can make everything possible. Together, we can join to become one, with one goal, one merged consciousness, and together, we can then enable a transcendence to a higher state, so not to leave anyone behind.

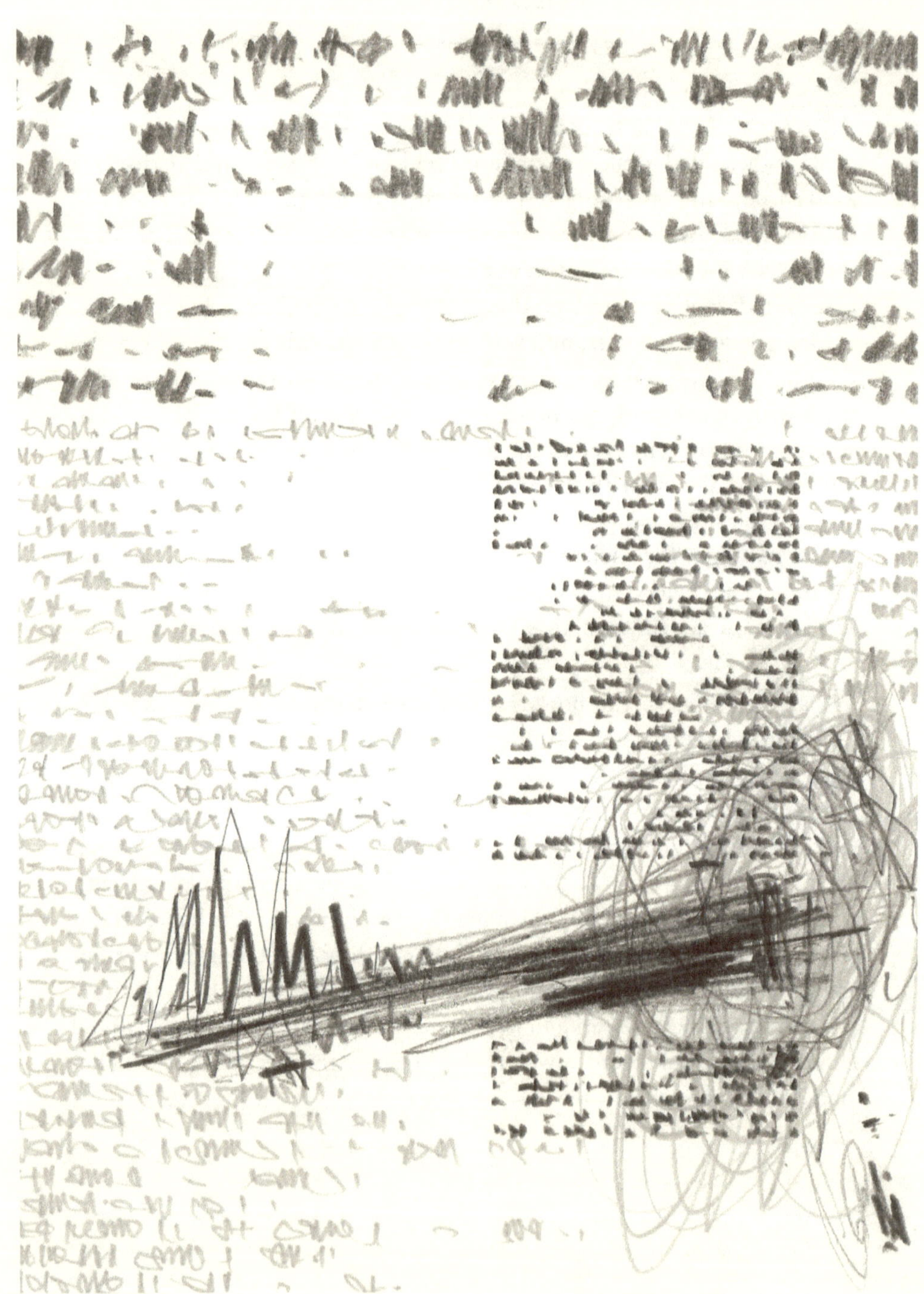

The Rise of the Asexual and Nonbinary

Our fate is to evolve as the ancients. At our end, our DNA will similarly corrupt and devolve into nothingness as the ancients. We must therefore decide whether we take the next step.

I remembered how Q had relayed the present dilemmas facing humanity, saying how rapidly evolution was changing our genetics, corrupting and morphing parts of our DNA. With such change, Q indicated that soon, we will be of no use to the ancients. Q added that we should thereby take care of what we have as we have special DNA that has the potential to help many.

Neither time nor evolution can stand still. Each will either progress or devolve, enhance, or corrupt. The latter is now occurring to our regenerative and reproductive abilities. The ancients had also faced this dilemma when time had begun to **corrupt** their DNA, which for them, then became a matter of survival. To persist, they searched for alternatives while extinction loomed. Something similar has started within us, placing us in a similar predicament.

We can already replicate ourselves in laboratories. We have the science, albeit a primitive form compared to the ancients. Our technology can be expanded so it can extend lifespans and synthesise our bodies. This is the science that can enable us to transcend our mortal form before our DNA fully corrupts beyond repair.

Cell morphing is already progressively changing and corrupting our DNA. Each year, every human cell undergoes twenty to fifty somatic mutations. This had enabled us rapidly to evolve but has since become lethal by it prematurely aging and corrupting cells, causing genetic mutations, illness, and death. This is despite us not having yet reached our ultimate form. In part, the ancients' manipulations caused this, with their tampering that enabled our lineage to bypass millions of otherwise necessary evolutionary time. Their tampering had begun the quickening process that cannot be halted or stopped, which is now rapidly taking us to an evolutionary end.

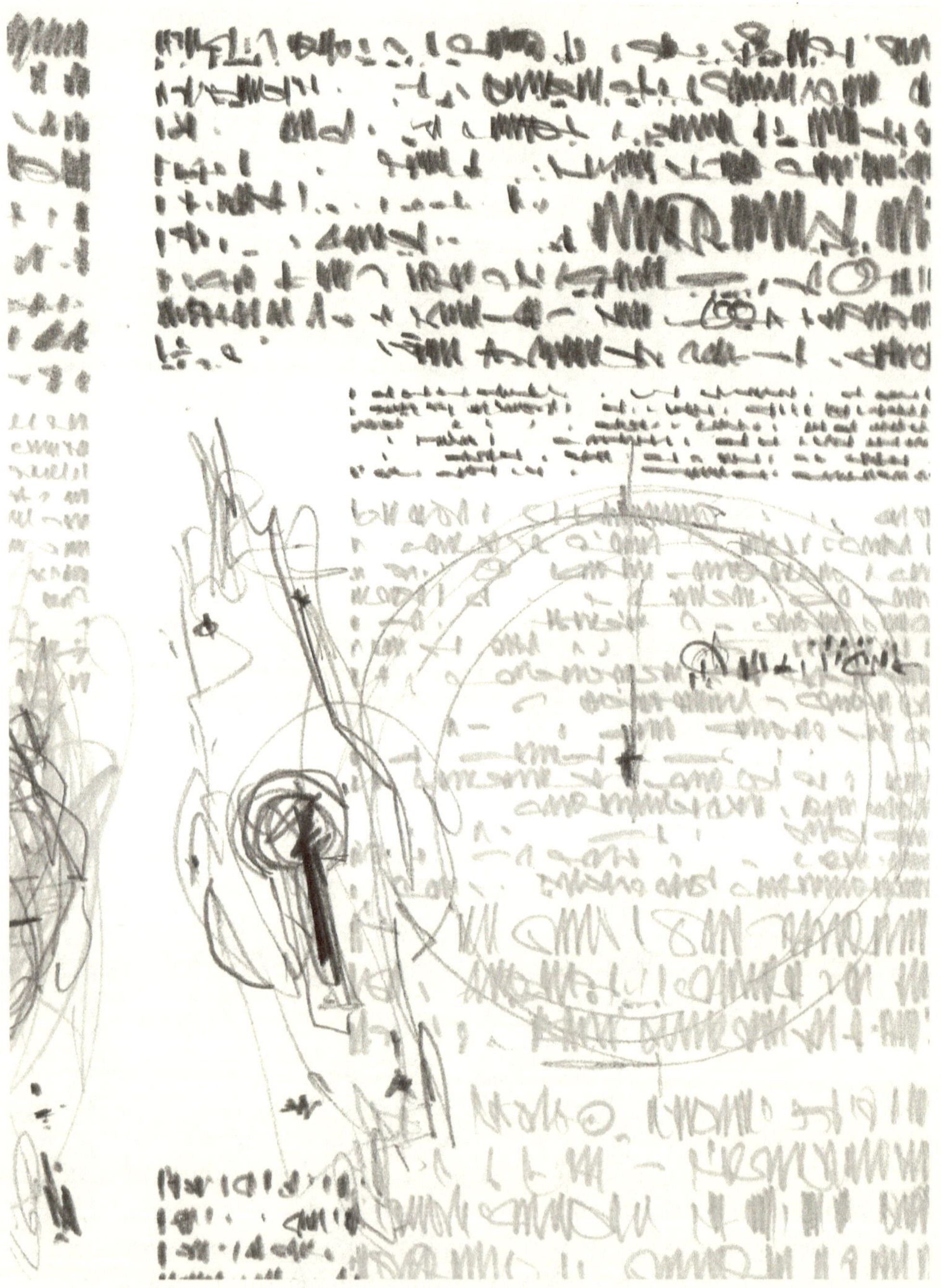

The Crossroads

As a race, we will soon reach a crossroads of sorts that will force us to decide which path we take.

At our end, our legacy carries forward consequences. We have caused climate change, and our meddling with Earth's biosphere has taken many species to the brink of another mass extinction, and yet we fail to acknowledge or rectify this. We do this as we are yet to control our greed for more or transcend past selfish desires. This, which has since placed life on Earth in peril, has driven us for eternity. This is what we do and who we are. Without change, the time to rectify this will soon pass.

Within us, a biological struggle has also commenced. This is mutating our cells, taking us to a time when the distinction between male and female will blur. This is exactly what happened to the ancients before their genetics began to devolve.

According to the U.S. CDC, 1 per cent of the human **population** is already asexual, and 2 per cent are unable to reproduce naturally. Assisted conception such as in vitro fertilisation technologies are already used worldwide. This has provided a short-term solution while hiding the larger and global infertility issue. To persist, we will need to regress back to some older or original human form, to when humans' DNA was more stable. With this, we might just be able to increase our lifespan and buy time to progress, reach a post human state, and attain immortality.

Whose World Is It?

Twelve million U.S. citizens believe the people in power, dressed in suits, are interstellar lizards. (Quote derived from Olga Oksman)

This is part of the ancients' legacy. They still exist and are with us. At times, they accompany us as we walk this Earth. In the heavens, they are omnipresent and all-powerful entities, having access to unlimited technologies and abilities. They are hundreds of millions of years old. To them, we are primitive yet to master our bodies or minds. We thereby are no match.

Having made us, they know who we are and all we are capable of. They now mostly watch us and, at times, help us as they still need us to maintain their form. They do this while remaining purposefully aloof, hiding from sight so not to scare us unnecessarily. When they do come, they change their synthetised form to human so they can mingle in our midst, work our systems and process, and influence what is to occur.

Other times, when they travel and we do happen to catch glimpses of them, all we see are **alien beings**, at times with UFOs high in the skies, deep in the oceans, or in outer space. They, however, are not aliens; nor are they visitors from other planets or places. These are the ancients, whose ancestors were born on Earth.

I remembered, when I left their out-of-place realm, being told our future is not certain. Another judgement day looms as the unthinkable is destined to reoccur. Then as the cycle of life turns, a darkness will envelop this world and push life to new limits. This will force change on all while a new era dawns. Only the ancients know what will happen, and undoubtedly, they have already safeguarded themselves, along with their interests and future.

Epilogue

This is a tale questioning creation along with our recorded history and all we believe to be true. This journey begins by lifting the veil on what kept the ancients hidden and secret. To do this, this tale unwinds history for all to see, including the deep, fathomless past. For some, this will awaken dormant thoughts and memories. For others, the surprising aspects of each revelation heightens the fear that the impossible could be a reality. This intriguing, nightmarish past with remembered glimpses of what once was then shatters all we believe. What emerges is filled with inextricable connections to age-old mysteries of the forgotten ancient race. Then by reflecting, a foretelling emerges with the unavoidable end of time.

There we find a stillness, a frozen Earth, a wasteland enveloped with heat and ice. Only Earth emerged triumphant, having succeeded, extinguishing all lifeforms from its surface. As time is then unwound, the past comes into focus. There, life thrives, with humans relentlessly trying to populate the surface while fighting a regression that devolves. This ends as Earth moves and shakes uncontrollably. Landscapes change as sea levels rapidly fall and then rise again. **Turmoil** ensues as blackness envelops before a brilliant, burning flash scorches the Earth. Life holds on, persisting while explosions spew lava on an already-molten surface. At its end, without reason, life then explodes with an exuberance and abundance. This, however, is short-lived as the cycle of life turns to begin to unravel all that existed. From this emerges triumphantly reptiles and dinosaurs, only to then be taken back to dust, replaced with another silent calmness. As the Earth heaves, it abruptly interrupts with its erupting lava spews that take life again to new limits, forcing all to struggle and adapt as a fluctuating climate then settles to freeze Earth. Trilobites and brachiopods briefly appear before time finally stops; Earth then begins to disintegrate. All that ever was momentarily floats, trying to coalesce in the vacuum of space, only to be ripped further apart and then pulled together, incessantly forced to collide until the ultimate explosion occurs. Everything then fades to nothingness.

The Book and Tale

Why are there so many seemingly unbelievable ancient myths with mysterious and strange tales that have persisted through time? Where does the truth in each lie?

This first asemic tale recalls a traumatic experience that turns into an insightful journey. What unfolds is supported with incomprehensible drawings that awaken the deep subconsciousness with further memory recalls. From these came the tale of an ancient time with a forgotten history and altered reality. The more that is read and deciphered, the more an otherwise **impossible** and unimaginable past emerges, one that has always existed. Within this tale, the many disjointed memory recalls bring forth their own arrangements that when combined, reveal the biggest and longest held secret.

These drawings and writings have always existed within our subconsciousness. We all carry some memory of these. Certain triggers and unrelated circumstances cause these to arise, linger, and often register in our thoughts. When studied, what emerges, however, are otherwise impossible suggestions that cannot readily be reconciled or fully understood. It is easier to dismiss and disregard rather than to question or challenge these. Nor is accepting a viable option, as this would then shatter everything, all we previously knew and believed, along with the reality and truths that kept society together. To confront this and make it palatable, each page of this book provides another chapter shedding new insight to an unfolding story that at its end, reveals the true mysteries of life on Earth.

Index

Eemian 95, 117, 127
Einstein, Albert xvii, 9, 207
equinoctial cycle 27
Europe 67, 145
Eve 93, 131
evolution xix, 29, 35, 37, 43, 85, 165, 185, 205, 209, 213, 215
extroversion 61

G

Ga 9, 15, 17, 23, 29, 41, 45, 51, 53, 55, 59, 153, 183
galactic year 27
Garden of Eden 93, 125, 131, 143, 153, 155, 171
gatekeeper 157, 207
genetics 43, 45, 73, 83, 91, 99, 101, 107, 119, 125, 131, 139, 141, 145, 155, 157, 159, 167, 169, 175, 197, 215, 217
glacial maximum 69, 95, 117, 135, 137
    last 95, 117, 135, 137, 167
glacial period, last 67, 95, 117, 127, 135
glaciation 51, 53, 55
Gondwanaland 25, 61
Great Dying 23, 25, 37, 43, 57, 59, 61, 73, 81, 105, 183
Great Oxidation Events 51, 55
greenhouse 25, 51, 55, 57, 63, 67, 69, 95, 117, 137
Gulf of Mexico 25

H

Holocene epoch 33, 67, 183, 185
hominins 9, 29, 65, 91, 117, 119, 121, 123, 125, 131, 143, 183
Homo sapiens 29, 123, 153, 205
Huronian Glaciation 53
hybridisation 45, 65, 121, 125

I

ice age:
    first 51, 55
    second 55
intelligence 3, 11, 15, 17, 19, 21, 37, 73, 77, 89, 91, 97, 99, 101, 103, 157, 205, 211
introversion 61
Isthmus of Panama 67

K

kalabtun 181, 183, 185
Karoo ice age 23
k'inchiltun 181

L

last universal common ancestor (LUCA) 23, 41, 45, 51, 183, 213
Late Cenozoic Ice Age 63, 67, 95, 117
Late Heavy Bombardment 51
Laurasia 25, 61
Long Count 181, 183, 185

M

Ma 9, 15, 17, 19, 23, 25, 27, 29, 31, 33, 35, 37, 41, 43, 45, 49, 51, 55, 57, 59, 61, 63, 65, 67, 73, 81, 85, 91, 95, 101, 105, 107, 117, 123, 131, 155, 165, 183, 185, 197
macro scales 99
mass extinctions:
    first 23, 51, 53, 57
    last 63, 65, 87, 91, 101
    late Devonian 23, 57, 183
    Ordovician-Silurian 23, 57, 183
    Precambrian and Vendian 23, 41, 55, 183
    Triassic-Jurassic 25, 43, 61, 183
Mayans 9, 159, 175, 179, 181, 185
Mediterranean Basin 67

V

volcanic activity 25, 37

Y

Yahweh 155, 175, 177
Younger Dryas 95, 117, 125, 127, 129,
          135, 137, 139, 149, 171, 175, 177,
          179, 187, 189, 191
Yucatán Peninsula 25, 179

Z

zodiac 27, 137

www.ingramcontent.com/pod-product-compliance
Lightning Source LLC
Chambersburg PA
CBHW051042250726
48656CB00001B/102